# PAPER
# CRAFT
# HOME

SARAH LOUISE MATTHEWS

# PAPER CRAFT HOME

25 BEAUTIFUL PROJECTS TO CUT, FOLD, AND SHAPE

BOULDER 2018

**Roost Books**
An imprint of Shambhala Publications, Inc.
4720 Walnut Street
Boulder, Colorado 80301
roostbooks.com

9 8 7 6 5 4 3 2 1

First U.S. Edition

Printed in China

Distributed in the United States by Penguin Random House LLC
and in Canada by Random House of Canada Ltd

Library of Congress Cataloging-in-Publication Data
Names: Matthews, Sarah Louise, author.
Title: Paper craft home: 25 beautiful projects to cut, fold, and
    shape / Sarah Louise Matthews.
Description: Boulder, Colorado: Roost Books, 2018. | Includes
    index.
Identifiers: LCCN 2017055554 | ISBN 9781611806090
(paperback)
Subjects: LCSH: Paper work. | BISAC: CRAFTS & HOBBIES /
    Papercrafts. | CRAFTS & HOBBIES / Decorating. | CRAFTS
    & HOBBIES / Stenciling.
Classification: LCC TT870 .M3735 2018 | DDC 745.54—dc23
LC record available at https://lccn.loc.gov/2017055554

Conceived, edited, and designed by
Quarto Publishing plc,
An imprint of The Quarto Group
The Old Brewery
6 Blundell Street
London N7 9BH

www.quartoknows.com

QUAR HOMG

**Senior Editors** Katie Crous and Claire Waite Brown
**Designer** Gemma Wilson
**Photography (step-by-step)** Sarah Lousie Matthews
**Photography (projects)** Simon Pask
**Creative Director** Moira Clinch
**Art Director** Caroline Guest
**Publisher** Sam Warrington

# CONTENTS

## THE PROJECTS 19

# INTRODUCTION

"Paper Engineer" would have been my dream job as a child, had I known of its existence—well, it would have been a close second after professional ballerina. I have been an avid maker for as long as I can remember, from my earliest memories folding origami penguins, cutting paper-doll chains, and covering myself in glitter, to now spending my days buried under paper in my studio in Sheffield, UK—cutting, folding, gluing, and interlocking to create innovative and playful paper designs.

I believe that paper is the most versatile crafting material. Truly accessible, it surrounds us in the form of cupcake liners, gift wrap, envelopes, greetings cards, and cardboard boxes, all of which are perfect to repurpose through crafting. Thanks to paper's universal availability, combined with the need for just a few basic tools, a small amount of space, and a bit of patience, I'm certainly not alone: paper craft is many people's introduction to crafting, be it folding paper airplanes, creating paper chains, or cutting paper snowflakes. I will never tire of the limitless possibilities a blank sheet offers, and I am endlessly fascinated with the unexpected ways in which paper can be cut, scored, creased, shaped, and glued to transform an everyday material into something extraordinary and precious. My paper love affair doesn't end at paper craft; I'm also obsessed with stationery, perfectly finished prints, and beautiful books, especially my little pop-up book collection.

Since graduating with a degree in textile surface design, I have designed and made cheerful, contemporary paper-cut stationery, decorations, and artwork, which I sell online, and worked with various brands and individual clients to create bespoke paper-engineered creations for photo shoots, visual merchandising, and events. The combination of a fully stocked plan chest, a brief that gets my brain ticking, and a hefty dose of imagination is my recipe for a dream workday, so I feel incredibly lucky to be on this journey, and I would love for you to join in through this book.

The following pages are filled with projects of ascending difficulty, so whether you are a novice taking your first paper-crafting steps or a seasoned pro, I hope you feel inspired to channel your creativity, set aside some time to slow down, and indulge in a "crafternoon" or two. The projects in this book are designed to be made with love and treasured for years to come, whether you want to create something beautiful for yourself or as a unique gift to make somebody's face light up with joy. I'd love to see what you make, so don't forget to share your creations with me @_sarah_matthews using #papercrafthome.

# ABOUT THIS BOOK

Thanks to paper's universal availability and the need for just a small number of basic tools, paper craft is the perfect introduction to crafting. Using just a few techniques, a blank sheet of paper can be transformed into something extraordinary and precious. In *Paper Craft Home*, Sarah Louise Matthews creates 25 unique projects that show off the versatility, beauty, and simplicity of paper.

## Technique used

Cutting
Scoring
Folding
Bow tying
Curling

## Skill level

Beginner          ● ○ ○
Intermediate      ● ● ○
Advanced          ● ● ●

All templates are at 100% unless otherwise indicated.

—— = cut

····· = score (mountain fold)

--- = score (valley fold)

## MATERIALS, TOOLS, AND BASIC TECHNIQUES (PAGES 10–17)

The book begins with a brief guide to the paper crafter's toolbox and an introduction to essential paper-craft skills, including cutting, scoring, and folding.

## THE PROJECTS (PAGES 19–125)

Organized in ascending order of skill, each project has step-by-step photography and easy-to-follow instructions.

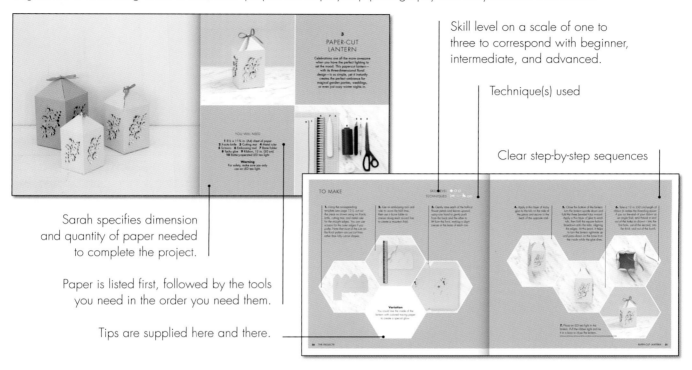

Skill level on a scale of one to three to correspond with beginner, intermediate, and advanced.

Technique(s) used

Clear step-by-step sequences

Sarah specifies dimension and quantity of paper needed to complete the project.

Paper is listed first, followed by the tools you need in the order you need them.

Tips are supplied here and there.

## THE TEMPLATES (PAGES 126–143)

This section contains templates to scan or trace for those projects that require them.

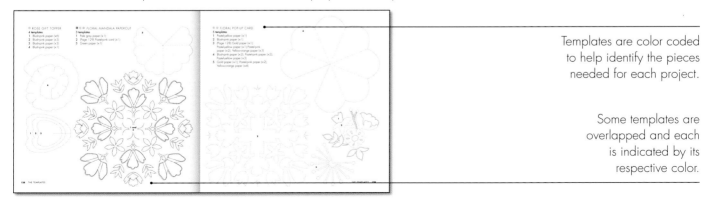

Templates are color coded to help identify the pieces needed for each project.

Some templates are overlapped and each is indicated by its respective color.

MATERIALS

## MATERIALS

*Must-have beginner materials

**1** Colored and
metallic papers*
I consider anything up to
around 60 lb (150 gsm) to
be paper rather than card.
Papers are easy to cut and
perfect for when you don't
need much strength.

**2** Colored and
metallic card—light
and heavy weights*
Anything that's 60–80 lb
(150–200 gsm) I consider to
be light card, and anything
above that to be card,
perfect for when you need
some durability and structure.

**3** Crepe papers
Available in light and heavy
weights for different projects,
crepe papers are gathered
to allow you to stretch and
shape them.

**4** Colored tissue paper
This very thin, lightweight
paper is perfect for making
tassels and pom-poms, and
using as packaging. Look
in gift wrap departments for
special patterned sheets.

**5** Tracing paper
and vellum
Translucent papers can be
found in a range of colors
and can be used in projects
for which you want a light,
delicate look.

**6** Foam board
Lightweight, easy to cut,
and available in a range of
thicknesses, use foam board
when your project needs
strength and/or depth.

**7** Washi tape
These fun, printed paper
tapes are available in a
variety of colors and patterns,
are used for decorative
purposes, and are easily
removed.

**8** Ribbon
I'm a ribbon hoarder, and
I cannot resist picking up
a special one when I spot
it. Ribbon is useful for gift
wrapping and creating
decorative fastenings on
projects.

**9** Paint
Any water-based paints, such
as acrylic paints, can be
used on paper and card.

**10** Floral wire
I use light-gauge floral wire
as stems for paper flowers
and leaves. A heavier
gauge might be used as
the structural element of the
project, perhaps for a wreath
or crown.

One of the best things about paper
craft is that you don't need an endless
list of expensive equipment, and
you may even already have some
of the essentials in your home.

TOOLS

## TOOLS

*Must-have beginner tools

**1** Scissors*
To extend their life, designate pairs for specific purposes, such as cutting paper/card, ribbon, or tape.

**2** X-acto knife*
My most-used tool, I use an X-acto knife, which is precise and gives the cleanest cuts. Remember to change the blade frequently.

**3** Metal ruler*
A metal ruler, or any ruler with a metal edge, is a must for cutting straight lines with an X-acto knife and when scoring lines with an embossing tool.

**4** Cutting mat*
Opt for a self-healing mat so that the surface bounces back after you cut into it.

**5** Embossing tool*
I use an embossing tool rather than my X-acto knife to create scored lines, eliminating the risk of accidentally cutting through your paper or card.

**6** Bone folder*
Use a bone folder to create sharp creases in your paper.

**7** Tacky glue*
My go-to adhesive, tacky glue is water-based, dries clear and flexible, and gives you some repositioning time.

**8** All-purpose adhesive (e.g., UHU glue)
This is stronger than tacky glue but can be more difficult to use as neatly, as it can spread quickly and dries with a more visible, high-gloss finish. I use this on areas where I want a stronger bond than tacky glue.

**9** Hot glue gun
Adhesive from a gun hardens almost instantly so is best suited to quite small areas where you want a fast bond (for example, attaching petals to a flower). Work quickly and accurately, as there is no time for repositioning.

**10** Double-sided tape
Generally not as strong as glue, this is handy for a quick, neat bond where strength is not vital.

**11** Floral tape
I use this to wrap around the stems of paper flowers. Floral tape needs to be pulled taut as you wrap to activate the adhesive.

**12** Stapler
This is perfect for speedily attaching multiple sheets of paper.

**13** Hole punch
Much easier than trying to cut tiny holes with an X-acto knife, having a range of punches will allow for different-sized holes.

**14** Pliers with wire cutters
Pliers with wire cutters come in handy for trimming wires, closing crimps, and grabbing small components.

**15** Tapestry needles
It is useful to have a mixture of needles with different-sized eyes for piercing holes and threading string/ribbon.

**16** Pencil and eraser*
Keep your pencil sharp for accurately marking measurements on paper or card.

**17** Paintbrushes
I like to keep a variety of different-sized paintbrushes, from fine-brushes for detailed work to 3 in. (8 cm) brushes to cover a large area.

# BASIC TECHNIQUES

## ✂ CUTTING

Cutting is the most frequently used technique in this book, needed for almost every project. If you are new to cutting with a knife, follow the instructions below and have a little practice before starting your first project.

**1.** For the neatest finish, photocopy the required template and attach it to the paper/card with removable tape such as washi tape. Alternatively, you can print a mirror image of the template directly onto the back of the paper/card; however, depending on how perfect your cutting is, some of the printed lines may be visible on the back of your project after cutting. Set up your workspace with a self-healing cutting mat, making sure that you have space around you to move your arms while you work.

**2.** Always begin with a new blade in your X-acto knife. It is important to change the blade regularly while you work to ensure clean cuts. Hold the X-acto knife like a pen, keeping the blade at a 45-degree angle. Always cut toward yourself, which gives you the most control over the knife and so is the safest way to work. Hold the paper with your other hand, rotating the paper as you work, to always cut toward your body.

**Tip**
If you feel more comfortable using scissors than an X-acto knife, use them to cut the outer edges of each shape.

**3.** When cutting straight lines, cut against a metal ruler for the cleanest cuts. Cut away from corners rather than into them, and begin with the most delicate, detailed part of the design, working your way through to the bigger shapes.

## --- SCORING AND ◣ FOLDING

Scoring is indenting the surface of the paper to prepare for clean, precise folds. It is good practice to score before every fold, but it's particularly important before folding card to give a neat finish.

**1.** A foolproof way of scoring is to use an embossing tool and ruler rather than an X-acto knife, as there is no risk of accidentally applying too much pressure and cutting through the paper. Work on a cutting mat, line the ruler up, then run the embossing tool alongside it, applying pressure to the surface of the paper. If you don't have an embossing tool, you can substitute it with a butter knife.

**2.** Refer to the template to confirm whether the fold should be a mountain or valley fold. On the templates in this book, mountain folds are indicated with a dotted line, and valley folds are indicated with a dashed line. The best way to remember the difference between the two is to think of the paper resembling a mountain or a valley. For a mountain fold, the crease creates a peak; for a valley fold, the crease creates a trough.

**3.** Use your fingers to make the fold, making sure it is positioned accurately along the prescored line, then pinch down in the center with your finger before flattening along to the edges.

**4.** Run the bone folder across the fold with even pressure to create a sharp crease.

# CURLING

Knowing how to curl paper is useful for mimicking natural shapes such as flower petals, and there are a few different ways to do it.

## Method 1: Scissors

**1.** Use scissors in a similar way to when retro curling ribbon. Take the piece of paper you want to curl, then select a pair of scissors with a blade length longer than the width of the paper.

**2.** Open the scissors. Hold the paper with one hand and the blade of the scissors below the paper in the other hand, with the thumb of that hand resting on top of the paper just ahead of the blade. Run the blade along the back of the paper, applying even pressure, all the way off the edge of the paper. Repeat, if required, to deepen the curl.

## Method 2: Wooden skewer

Use a wooden skewer in a similar way to the scissors. This method is a good one for children to try (under supervision) as an alternative to using the scissor blade. Hold the paper with one hand and the skewer below the paper in the other hand, with the thumb of that hand resting on top of the paper just ahead of the skewer. Run the skewer along the back of the paper, applying even pressure, all the way off the edge of the paper. Repeat, if required, to deepen the curl.

## Method 3: Cylinder

Roll the paper around a cylindrical object. Select a cylinder with a small diameter, such as a wooden skewer for small pieces of paper / tighter curls, or a larger diameter, such as a marker, for larger pieces / looser curls. Simply roll the paper around the cylinder, squeeze slightly to keep the shape, then unroll.

## ∞ BOW TYING

Ribbon fastenings are a recurring theme throughout this book, and knowing how to tie the perfect bow is an invaluable skill to use for the perfect finishing touch to your projects and gifts.

**1.** Make sure you have a manageable amount of overhanging ribbon on either side of where the bow will be. Begin by tying a knot. There will now be one end of the ribbon at the top and one at the bottom. Always make your first bow loop using the bottom length of ribbon. This loop will become the right half of the bow, so pull it up and to the right so it is in the correct position.

**2.** Take the upper length of ribbon and pull it down over the top of the first loop. Push the section closest to the center behind the first loop, toward the left, to create the second loop.

**3.** To create an even bow shape, begin with loops smaller than you want them to be. Put one thumb through each loop, then use your index and middle fingers to hold the tail ends of the bow against the back of the base of your thumbs, but not so tightly that the tail ends can't move. Evenly pull your thumbs outward until you achieve the desired size, allowing the tails to run behind your hands and wiggling to get the bow in position.

**4.** Remove your thumbs, keeping the loops nicely rounded, and cut the tail ends to even lengths with either single or double-pointed ends. To cut double-pointed ends, fold the ribbon in half along the width, then make a diagonal cut from the outer edges up toward the fold.

### Tying single-sided ribbon

It is easiest to use a double-sided ribbon (a ribbon that looks the same on both sides), but if you want to use a single-sided ribbon, make sure your first loop is right-side out. When you pull the top end down and over, make sure that the right side of the ribbon faces outward (make a twist if necessary), then make a twist in the ribbon when you pass it behind the first loop. This will mean that your second loop will also be right-side out. Make another twist in the ribbon at the center point between the second loop and the tail (see Step 3, above).

# THE PROJECTS

# 1

# FLORAL MANDALA PAPERCUT

This floral mandala papercut is an explosion of color, repetition, and symmetry, created through cut and layered papers, and with folded elements to add texture. The geometrically organized shapes of mandalas are calming to look at, and, if you have an eye for geometry and florals alike, then this is the perfect project to hone your paper-cutting skills.

## YOU WILL NEED

9 × 9 in. (23 × 23 cm) sheet of paper in:
**1** yellow   **2** green   **3** pink
**4** pale gray   **5** X-acto knife   **6** Metal ruler
**7** Cutting mat   **8** Bone folder
**9** Double-sided tape

# TO MAKE

**1.** Use an X-acto knife, metal ruler, and cutting mat to trim the yellow paper to 8 × 8 in. (21 × 21 cm).

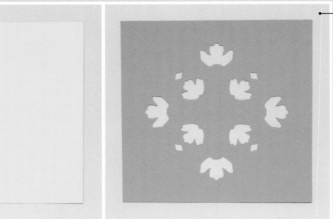

**2.** Using the corresponding template (see page 128), cut out the green piece as shown.

**3.** Using the corresponding templates (pages 128–129), cut out the pastel-pink piece and then the pale gray piece as shown. Note that some of the cuts are just cut lines rather than fully cut-out shapes.

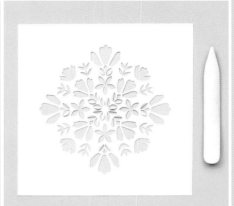

**4.** Take the gray sheet and gently fold each of the half-cut leaves back on itself, then flatten with a bone folder.

**5.** Take the pink piece and place the gray piece on top, aligning the cuts. Gently pushing from the back, raise each of the half-cut pink flower petals upward through the corresponding holes in the gray sheet. This time, instead of folding back and flattening the creases with a bone folder, use your fingers to gently lift the petals upward.

**6.** Cut four pieces of double-sided tape and attach them between the layers, one in each corner, to secure the layers together. Then, using double-sided tape, attach the green piece to the back of the gray and pink sheets, aligning the cuts.

**7.** Attach the yellow piece to the back using double-sided tape. Use the metal ruler, X-acto knife, and cutting mat to trim any uneven edges.

## 2

# BOTANICAL MONOGRAM

With the arrival of spring comes the lust for botanical accents around the home. If you don't have naturally green fingers, this cute monogram, with its mixture of gorgeous green leaves and pink buds, is the perfect way to add a botanical touch to your decor.

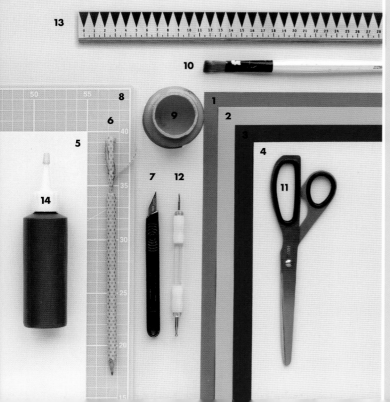

## YOU WILL NEED

5¾ × 8¼ in. (A5) sheet of paper in:
**1** medium green   **2** light green
**3** dark green   **4** pink
**5** 8¼ × 11¾ in. (A4) sheet of foam board
**6** Pencil   **7** X-acto knife   **8** Cutting mat
**9** Green acrylic paint   **10** Paintbrush
**11** Scissors   **12** Embossing tool
**13** Metal ruler   **14** Tacky glue

# TO MAKE

**1.** Use a pencil to draw out your own letter onto the foam board and an X-acto knife and cutting mat to cut it out.

**2.** Paint the front and sides of your foam board letter using green paint.

**3.** Using the corresponding templates (see page 137), cut out a selection of leaves from all three green papers, using the X-acto knife or scissors.

**4.** Use an embossing tool and ruler to score the leaves with the fold lines marked on the templates. Turn the leaves over and make mountain folds on the back. Work on the leaves one at a time, using the side of one finger to push from behind and the other hand to gently squeeze either side of each leaf. When you turn the leaves back the right way, they will have neat valley folds.

**5.** Using the corresponding templates, cut out eight stem pieces from green paper and 16 bud pieces from pink paper. Apply a small amount of tacky glue to the back of the bud ends of the stem pieces, and press the pink bud pieces onto the glue.

**6.** Use tacky glue to fix the leaves and stems to the front of the letter, trying to cover the foam board as much as you can. Where possible, overlap the pieces so that the stem of each sprig is covered by the next leaf.

# 3
# PAPER-CUT LANTERN

Celebrations are all the more awesome when you have the perfect lighting to set the mood. This paper-cut lantern—with its three-dimensional floral design—is so simple, yet it instantly creates the perfect ambience for magical garden parties, weddings, or even just cozy winter nights in.

## YOU WILL NEED

**1** 8¼ × 11¾ in. (A4) sheet of paper
**2** X-acto knife   **3** Cutting mat   **4** Metal ruler
**5** Scissors   **6** Embossing tool   **7** Bone folder
**8** Tacky glue   **9** Ribbon, 12 in. (30 cm)
**10** Battery-operated LED tea light

### Warning
For safety, make sure you only
use an LED tea light.

# TO MAKE

**1.** Using the corresponding template (see page 131), cut out the piece as shown using an X-acto knife, cutting mat, and metal ruler for the straight edges. You can use scissors for the outer edges if you prefer. Note that most of the cuts on the floral pattern are just cut lines rather than fully cut-out shapes.

**2.** Use an embossing tool and ruler to score the fold lines, then use a bone folder to crease along each scored line to create a mountain fold.

**3.** Gently raise each of the half-cut flower petals and leaves upward, using one hand to gently push from the back and the other to lift from the front, making a slight crease at the base of each one.

**Variation**
You could line the inside of the lantern with colored tracing paper to create a special glow.

**4.** Apply a thin layer of tacky glue to the tab on the side of the piece and secure to the back of the opposite end.

**5.** Close the bottom of the lantern: turn the lantern upside down and fold the three beveled tabs inward. Apply a thin layer of glue to each tab, then fold the square bottom facedown onto the tabs, aligning the edges. At this point, it helps to turn the lantern right-side up and press down on the base from the inside while the glue dries.

**6.** Take a 12 in. (30 cm) length of ribbon (it makes the threading easier if you cut the end of your ribbon at an angle first), and thread in and out of the holes as shown—into the first hole, out of the second, into the third, and out of the fourth.

**7.** Place an LED tea light in the lantern. Pull the ribbon tight and tie it in a bow to close the lantern.

# 4

# HOUSE GIFT BOX

This gift box is simple yet utterly adorable. Once you familiarize yourself with the process for making one, why not try making a whole town? For instance, 24 miniature house gift boxes—numbered and each filled with a little treat—could create an Advent town, and be a keepsake to treasure year after year.

## YOU WILL NEED

**1** 8¼ × 11¾ in. (A4) sheet of light card in marble
**2** 5¾ × 8¼ in. (A5) sheet of paper in gold
**3** X-acto knife  **4** Cutting mat  **5** Metal ruler
**6** Scissors  **7** Embossing tool
**8** Bone folder  **9** Tacky glue
**10** Tissue paper, 8 × 8 in. (20 × 20 cm)
**11** Ribbon, 12 in. (30 cm)

# TO MAKE

**1.** Using the corresponding templates (see page 137), cut out each piece as shown with an X-acto knife, cutting mat, and metal ruler for the straight edges. You could use scissors for the outer edges if you prefer.

**2.** Use an embossing tool and ruler to score the fold lines. Use a bone folder to crease along each score line to make a mountain fold.

**3.** Apply a thin layer of tacky glue to the tab on the side of the marble piece and secure to the back of the opposite end, flattening the piece in half while the glue begins to dry.

**4.** Form the three-dimensional house shape and turn it upside down so that the roof is pointing downward. Close the base of the box, folding the sides inward in the numerical order shown on the template. When you fold in the final piece, push it down until the tab tucks itself under the other pieces. You will need to push it quite far, and it will look like everything is caving inward, but it will suddenly slot into place.

**5.** Sort the smaller gold scalloped strips into those with full-scalloped edges and those with half-scalloped edges. Take a strip with half-scalloped edges and apply a line of glue along the back of the long straight edge. Attach the strip to one of the large gold pieces, positioning it so that the center of each scallop on the strip is aligned with the tip of the cut between the two scallops below. Continue this process, alternating between the two types of strip until you reach the top of the piece. Try to align the top of the final strip with the top of the backing piece. Repeat with the remaining gold pieces to create two identical roof pieces.

**6.** Take the marble house piece and apply a thin layer of glue to the outside of one of the roof sections, avoiding the semicircle loop. Take the first gold roof piece and press onto the glue, aligning the top of the two pieces. The semicircle should stick off the top, while the side and bottom edges of the gold piece should overhang the marble. Immediately, while the glue is still wet, turn it around so that you can see the back, and check that the gold piece is central, altering the position to even out the overhang on the side edges if required. Repeat for the second roof piece.

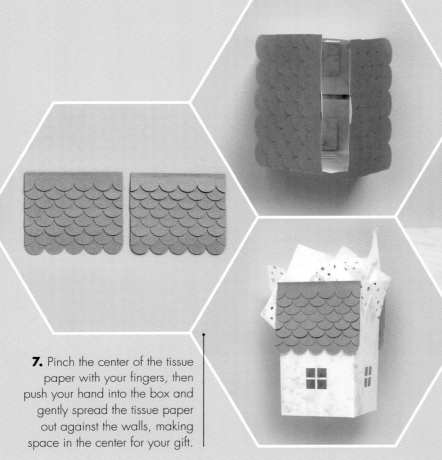

**7.** Pinch the center of the tissue paper with your fingers, then push your hand into the box and gently spread the tissue paper out against the walls, making space in the center for your gift.

**8.** Fill the box with your gift, then thread the ribbon through the two semicircle loops and tie in a knot to close the box. Finish by tying a bow.

# 5

# MINIMAL VASE

I'm pretty confident that I'm not alone in listing flowers as one of my favorite things, and this simple geometric vase is the perfect way to display your beloved blooms. It is totally functional thanks to the glass inside, which can be filled with water to keep your flowers fresh, or skip the water and fill it with paper flowers to create an everlasting floral display.

## YOU WILL NEED

**1** 11¾ × 16½ in. (A3) sheet of light card
**2** X-acto knife   **3** Cutting mat   **4** Metal ruler
**5** Scissors   **6** Embossing tool
**7** Bone folder   **8** Tacky glue
**9** Small glass

# TO MAKE

**1.** Using the template (see page 141), cut out the shape using an X-acto knife, cutting mat, and metal ruler, or scissors if you prefer.

**2.** Use an embossing tool and ruler to score the fold lines.

**3.** Use a bone folder to fold each scored line into a mountain fold.

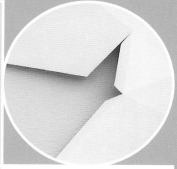

## Tip

You could also use this as a pen pot, makeup brush pot, or even a plant pot (just remember to add pebbles to the bottom of the glass for drainage).

**4.** Turn the creased piece over so that you are working on the back and the folds are now valley folds. Each section that splays out from the center has two tabs down one side. Work around the piece, applying a thin layer of tacky glue to the back of each tab, before attaching it to the front of the adjacent edge, aligning the crease of the tabbed piece with the edge of the adjacent side.

**5.** Place your glass in the paper vase, then just add water and fresh flowers!

# 6

# FLORAL FAIRY LIGHTS

There's something so cozy about the soft glow of fairy lights. This sweet design works for all seasons, and the project is simple. The lights reflect on the metallic paper in the dark, and they also make a gorgeous garland, looking just as sweet when turned off!

## YOU WILL NEED

8¼ × 11¾ in. (A4) sheet of single-sided mirror paper in: **1** gold **2** copper
**3** X-acto knife **4** Cutting mat **5** Scissors
**6** String of 10 LED fairy lights
**7** All-purpose adhesive **8** Bone folder

### Warning
For safety, make sure you only use LED fairy lights.

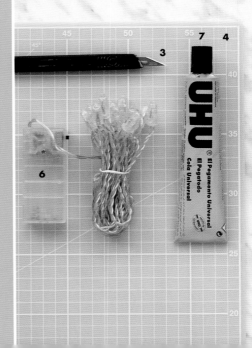

# TO MAKE

**1.** Using the corresponding templates (see page 131), cut out the flower and leaf pieces as shown using an X-acto knife and a cutting mat, or scissors if you prefer.

**2.** Take the flower pieces, one at a time and with the metallic side facing up. Use the blade of your scissors to gently curl each individual petal tip backward.

**3.** Wrap each flower around a fairy light, white side facing out, alternating between the two colors. Overlap and glue the two end petals, aligning the edges. If the flower is a little loose around the light, apply a dot of glue to the base.

**4.** Use a bone folder to fold each leaf piece in half, metallic side facing out.

**5.** Wrap the leaves around the fairy-light cable, in between the flowers. Glue the two halves of each leaf together, sandwiching the wire against the fold.

# 7
# SWAN GIFT BAG

Swans are beautiful—from their clean white feathers and beak's flash of orange and black to their whimsical elegance and poise. No matter where your love of swans stems from (for me, it was playing a cygnet in the ballet at age six), this project will reignite that admiration while providing a stylish gift bag.

## YOU WILL NEED

**1** 2 11¾ × 16½ in. (A3)
sheets of paper in white
5¾ × 8¼ in. (A5) sheet of paper in:
**2** black   **3** coral
**4** X-acto knife   **5** Cutting mat
**6** Metal ruler   **7** Scissors
**8** Embossing tool   **9** Set square
**10** Bone folder   **11** Tacky glue

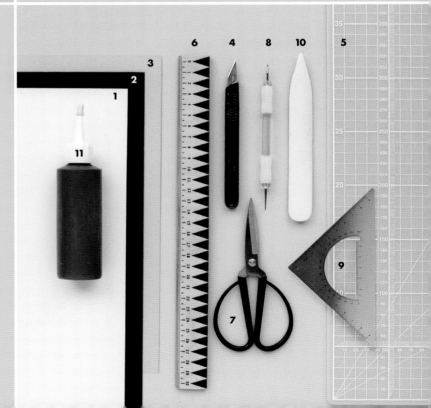

# TO MAKE

**1.** Using the corresponding templates (see page 135), cut out each piece as shown with an X-acto knife, cutting mat, and metal ruler where necessary, or scissors for the outer cuts if you prefer.

**2.** Use an embossing tool and ruler to score the fold lines. It is helpful to use a set square (or other right-angled object) lined up with the cut edges and other score lines to accurately score the 45-degree lines on the two side panels as shown. Use a bone folder to fold each score line into a mountain or valley fold according to the markings on the template.

**3.** Apply a thin layer of tacky glue to the folded tab down the right-hand side of the bag piece and attach it to the back of the opposite edge.

**4.** To close the bottom of the bag, begin by folding the side tabs inward. Take the first beveled tab and apply glue in the areas where it will overlap the side tabs. Repeat this for the remaining beveled tab, applying glue where it will overlap, before closing to seal the base of the bag. At this point, it helps to turn the bag right-side up and press down on the base of the bag from the inside to secure it while the glue dries.

**5.** Place the bag in front of you so that the upward-facing side has the head section of the handle on the left-hand side of the bag as shown. Take the larger feathered strip piece and apply a line of glue to the back of the top edge, then attach it to the front of the bag, aligning the vertical and horizontal straight edges of the piece with the side and base of the bag.

**6.** Take the second feathered strip piece and apply a line of glue to the back of the top edge, then attach it to the front of the bag, aligning the vertical straight edges of the piece with the left and right edges of the bag, and the tips of the feathers with the tops of the previous row's feathers.

**7.** Take the feathered neck piece and apply a line of glue around the edge, avoiding the feathered edge and the head so that the feathers and head will be loose, giving the bag dimension and texture. Press the neck piece onto the bag, aligning the edges. Once the glue has dried, gently use your fingers to slightly curve the end of the swan's head and neck upward.

**8.** Glue the black beak piece onto the coral beak piece in the position shown. The black piece will overhang the coral slightly. Glue the eye end of the beak piece to the head of the swan as shown: first, hold the beak on the head to work out where to apply the glue, then apply a thin layer of glue to the overlapping area and press onto the swan's head.

# 8

# CHERRY BLOSSOM TWIGS

Blossom season is one of my favorite times of the year. There's nothing quite like strolling beneath a beautiful mass of cotton candy–pink flowers as their petals drop like confetti. The season is soon over, but this pretty project will make it last all year.

## YOU WILL NEED

8¼ × 11¾ in. (A4) sheet of paper in:
**1** dark red **2** blush pink **3** pastel pink
**4** Sheet of tissue paper in pink
**5** X-acto knife **6** Cutting mat **7** Scissors
**8** Tacky glue **9** Wooden skewer
**10** Polystyrene balls, ⅖ in. (1 cm) diameter
(see Preparation [page 48] for guide
to quantity) **11** Tapestry needle
**12** Twigs **13** Hot glue gun

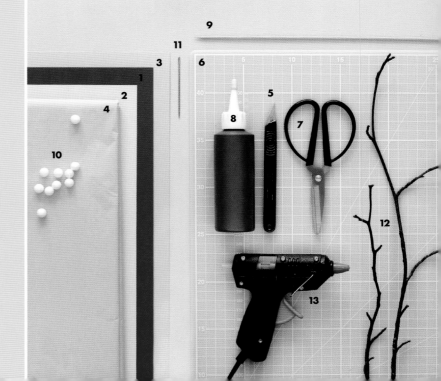

# TO MAKE

**1.** Using the corresponding templates (see page 139), cut out a handful of dark red cross-shaped pieces, blush-pink and pastel-pink flower pieces, and one small, dark red star-shaped piece for each flower-shaped piece, using an X-acto knife and a cutting mat, or scissors if you prefer.

**2.** Use tacky glue to attach one red star-shaped piece to the center of each flower piece.

**3.** Place a wooden skewer over the center of the first flower petal, then use your fingers to wrap the petal around the stick, squeezing and rolling the paper between your fingers to keep the shape; then let go. Repeat for each petal on every flower.

**4.** Cut out squares of pink tissue paper large enough to wrap around the polystyrene balls. Apply a small amount of tacky glue around the edge of the first piece of tissue paper, as well as a few dots of glue in the center, then wrap the tissue around a polystyrene ball. Try to keep one side as smooth as possible, and twist the excess paper into a stalk.

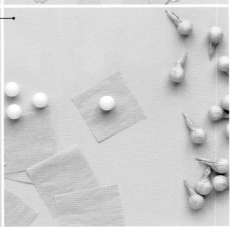

### Preparation

Before you start, count the number of twig ends on your stick, as this is the maximum number of buds (balls) you will need to make. The number of flowers you make is up to you.

**5.** Use scissors to trim off the tissue-paper stalks as close to the ball as you can.

**6.** Take the first red cross-shaped piece and apply a thin layer of tacky glue to the back. Press it onto the first tissue-wrapped ball, covering the area where the stalk was cut off and wrapping the points up around the sides of the ball. Repeat for all tissue balls, then leave to dry.

**7.** Use a tapestry needle to make a hole in one side of each ball, through the center of the red cross. Don't pierce all the way through, only halfway. Apply a dot of tacky glue to the end of each twig end and push a ball onto each twig.

**8.** Use a glue gun to apply a dot of hot glue to the back of your first flower, then press it onto the stick. Repeat with all remaining flowers, arranging thems in clusters.

# 9
# FLOWER PENCIL TOPPER

Chances are, if you're into paper cutting, you're probably also a stationery addict. If you can't resist a pretty ruler or quirky pair of scissors, and you have an ever-growing collection of pens and pencils, this project is for you. It's a combination of two of my favorite things — stationery and flowers. This pencil topper will look adorable poking out of your pen pot, and it will make you smile every time you reach for it.

## YOU WILL NEED

5¾ × 8¼ in. (A5) sheet of paper in:
**1** blue   **2** pale blue   **3** copper
**4** X-acto knife   **5** Cutting mat   **6** Scissors
**7** Embossing tool   **8** Metal ruler
**9** Bone folder   **10** Tacky glue   **11** Pencil

# TO MAKE

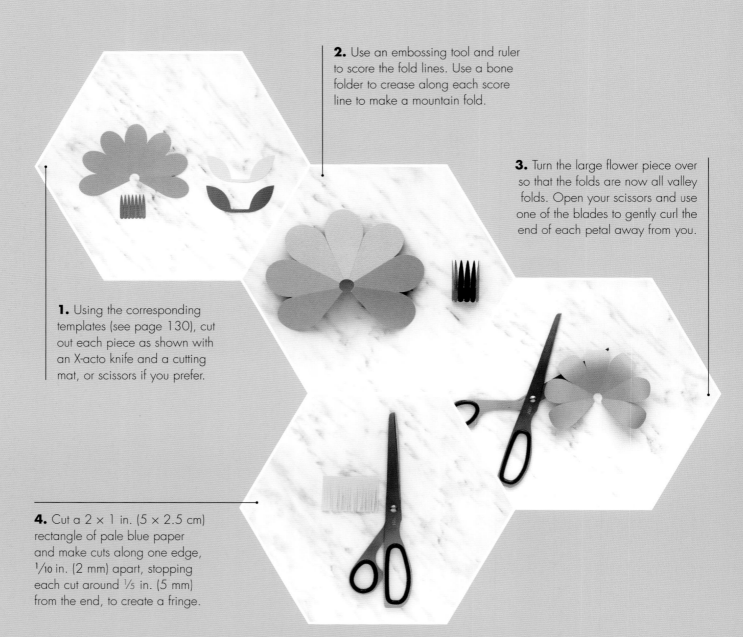

**2.** Use an embossing tool and ruler to score the fold lines. Use a bone folder to crease along each score line to make a mountain fold.

**3.** Turn the large flower piece over so that the folds are now all valley folds. Open your scissors and use one of the blades to gently curl the end of each petal away from you.

**1.** Using the corresponding templates (see page 130), cut out each piece as shown with an X-acto knife and a cutting mat, or scissors if you prefer.

**4.** Cut a 2 × 1 in. (5 × 2.5 cm) rectangle of pale blue paper and make cuts along one edge, 1/10 in. (2 mm) apart, stopping each cut around 1/5 in. (5 mm) from the end, to create a fringe.

**5.** Apply a line of tacky glue along the base of your fringed piece, and wrap the piece around the top of your pencil so that the fringe overhangs the top. Hold in place while the glue begins to dry.

**6.** Take the large flower piece and apply a thin layer of glue to the front of one of the end petals. Wrap the piece around the pencil, then overlap the two end petals, aligning the edges, and press to secure around the pencil. Push the flower up the pencil to meet the base of the fringe.

**7.** Take the jagged copper piece and apply a thin layer of glue all over the back. Wrap it around the pencil to cover the join between the flower and the pencil, positioning it so that one of the long copper triangles is central on the back of each flower petal. Overlap one end section of the copper piece with the other end, aligning the edges.

**8.** Take the first leaf piece and apply a thin layer of glue to the back of one of the leaf sections and the central strip area. Wrap it around the pencil, then align the two leaf shapes and press together while the glue begins to dry. Repeat with the second leaf.

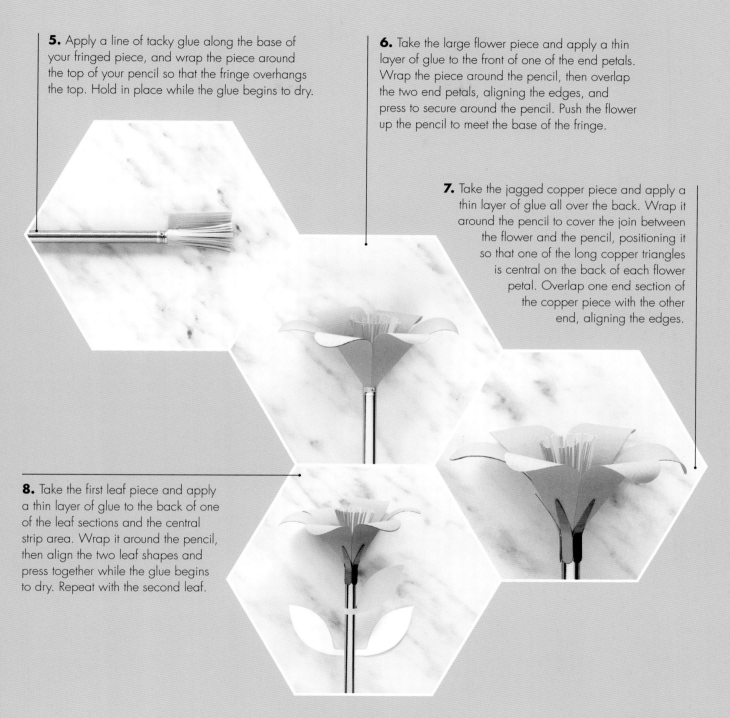

# 10

# FLORAL CAKE TOPPERS

The attractive translucent paper vellum, made from rag or plasticized cotton, is available in a range of colors and can create beautiful effects in paper cutting. It gives these cake toppers an elegant edge, while adding a fun element to your party table.

## YOU WILL NEED

8¼ × 11¾ in. (A4) sheet of vellum in:
**1** yellow  **2** green  **3** blue
**4** white  **5** pink
Sheet of tissue paper in:
**6** pink  **7** blue  **8** yellow
**9** X-acto knife  **10** Cutting mat  **11** Scissors
**12** Bone folder  **13** Metal ruler
**14** Tacky glue  **15** Wooden skewers

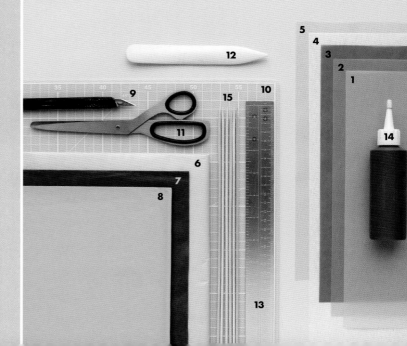

# TO MAKE

**1.** Using the corresponding templates (see page 143), cut out the flower pieces from colored vellums and the leaves from green vellum. Use an X-acto knife and a cutting mat, or scissors if you prefer. You will need one of each of the flower templates for each cake topper.

**2.** Score the fold lines on the leaves. For vellum, an X-acto knife works better than an embossing tool. To score, run the blade lightly over the paper.

**3.** Each scored line needs to be folded to form a valley fold: turn the leaves over so that you are working on the back—you will now need to make mountain folds so that when you turn it back the right way they will be valley folds. Use the side of one finger to push from behind and the other hand to gently squeeze either side of each leaf to form the mountain fold. Repeat with every leaf, then put the folded leaf pieces to one side.

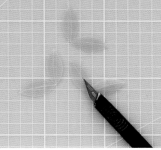

## Hone your skills

When scoring with the X-acto knife, be careful not to apply pressure and accidentally cut through the paper.

**4.** Use a bone folder to fold each flower piece in half, then open to make a valley fold. Turn 90 degrees and fold in half again, then unfold to make a second valley fold.

**5.** Turn each flower over so that the valley folds are now mountain folds. Again, fold in half, then unfold to make a valley. Turn 90 degrees and fold in half again, then unfold to make another valley fold. The flower should now have rotational folds, alternating between mountain and valley folds.

**6.** Squeeze each flower, encouraging the mountain folds together to meet in the center to create the shape shown.

**7.** Cut one 3 × 1½ in. (8 × 4 cm) rectangle of tissue paper for each cake topper. Use scissors to fringe along one edge, making cuts every ⅕ in. (5 mm) and cutting down to around ¼ in. (7 mm) from the end.

**8.** Apply a line of tacky glue along the base of each fringed piece before wrapping around the end of a wooden skewer.

**9.** Take the folded flower pieces and cut a tiny bit off each center point, just enough so that the skewer fits snugly through the center.

**10.** Take the flowers with thin petals and the fringed skewers. Apply a line of glue around the base of the tissue fringe, then push the flower up from the bottom of the skewer to meet the glued line.

**11.** Apply a line of glue around the skewer, just below the first flower. Push a flower with larger petals up from the bottom of the skewer through the glue to meet the base of the previous flower.

**12.** Apply a dot of glue to the back center of each pair of leaves and press onto the skewer. Attach either one or two pairs of leaves to each stick.

# 11

# ROSE GIFT TOPPER

Gift wrapping can be a very rewarding pastime: when you've spent so long choosing the perfect gift, it only seems right to wrap it with the care it deserves and make someone feel extra special. This beautiful paper rose gift topper is a present in itself and the perfect addition to take your gifting game up a notch.

## YOU WILL NEED

**1** 8¼ × 11¾ in. (A4) sheet of paper in blush pink
**2** X-acto knife  **3** Cutting mat  **4** Scissors
**5** Wooden skewer  **6** Hot glue gun

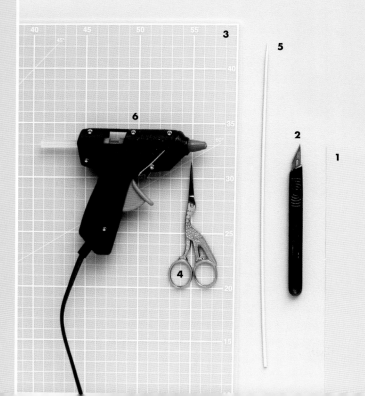

# TO MAKE

SKILL LEVEL ●●○
TECHNIQUES ✄ ◎

**1.** Using the corresponding templates (see page 128), cut out each piece as shown with an X-acto knife and a cutting mat, or scissors if you prefer.

**2.** Take the spiral piece. Starting at the outer end, roll it around a wooden skewer, squeeze to keep the shape, and then let go.

**3.** The spiral piece has eight petal sections, beginning at the outer end. Open your scissors and use the blade to gently curl back the end of each petal.

## Hone your skills

When using a glue gun, you need to work fast, as the glue hardens really quickly!

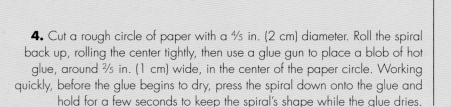

**4.** Cut a rough circle of paper with a $\frac{4}{5}$ in. (2 cm) diameter. Roll the spiral back up, rolling the center tightly, then use a glue gun to place a blob of hot glue, around $\frac{2}{5}$ in. (1 cm) wide, in the center of the paper circle. Working quickly, before the glue begins to dry, press the spiral down onto the glue and hold for a few seconds to keep the spiral's shape while the glue dries.

**5.** Once dry, trim away any excess paper circle around the base of the glued spiral.

**6.** Take each of the individual petals and use the blade of your scissors to gently curl the petal tips back.

**7.** Take your first petal. Use the glue gun to apply a small amount of glue along one edge of the cut line up the base of the petal. Working quickly, before the glue dries, overlap the two sides of the cut line, to give the petal a cupped shape, and hold for a couple of seconds while the glue dries. Repeat for all remaining petals.

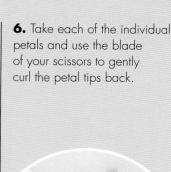

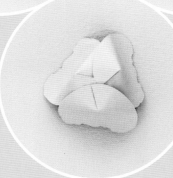

**8.** Separate the petals into small (three), medium (three), and large (six) petals. Begin with the small petals. Turn the glued spiral upside down, then use the glue gun to apply a blob of glue to the top of the base of the first petal, before quickly turning the petal upside down and positioning on the back of the glued spiral. Repeat this with the remaining two small petals, arranging them so that they are equally spaced around the spiral.

**9.** Repeat Step 8, but this time with the three medium petals, positioning each one in between two small petals.

**10.** Repeat Step 8 again with the large petals, gluing the petals in two layers of three, each time arranging the large petal between the petals of the previous layer.

# TO MAKE

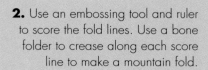

**1.** Using the corresponding templates (see page 130), cut out the marble piece as shown with an X-acto knife, cutting mat, and metal ruler where necessary, or use scissors if you prefer.

**2.** Use an embossing tool and ruler to score the fold lines. Use a bone folder to crease along each score line to make a mountain fold.

**3.** Place the creased piece in front of you, right-side up. Along the bottom is a row of triangle shapes, each with a tab along its right-hand edge. Work along the row, applying a thin layer of tacky glue to the front of each tab, before attaching it to the back of the adjacent edge on the next triangle. Once you have worked all the way along the piece joining each triangle to the next, apply glue to the two end tabs and attach them to the back of the opposite edge of the piece.

**4.** Using the template, cut out three triangle shapes in each color. Apply a thin layer of glue to the back of each shape and attach it to the outside faces of the marble piece, leaving the marble paper exposed on some faces. It is a good idea to plan out the positions of your colored triangles before you start gluing. You could use adhesive putty to temporarily position them while you plan your layout.

# 14

# FLORAL POP-UP CARD

There is something so magical about pop-up cards. I have the most vivid memory of spending hours meticulously making a pop-up bunny card from a craft book when I was tiny and being completely blown away when it worked, opening and closing it with amazement. Designed to surprise, this card blooms into a gorgeous three-dimensional bouquet when opened. It looks impressive, but is surprisingly straightforward to make.

## YOU WILL NEED

8¼ × 11¾ in. (A4) sheet of paper in:
**1** pastel pink   **2** pale nude   **3** pastel yellow
2 8¼ × 11¾ in. (A4) sheets of paper in:
**4** blush pink   **5** yellow orange
**6** 5¾ × 8¼ in. (A5) sheet of single-sided mirror paper in gold
**7** X-acto knife   * Cutting mat (not pictured)
**8** Scissors   **9** Metal ruler
**10** Embossing tool   **11** Bone folder
**12** Tacky glue

# TO MAKE

**1.** Using the corresponding templates (see pages 128–129), cut out each piece as shown with an X-acto knife and a cutting mat. Also cut out two 10 × 5 in. (25 × 12.5 cm) pieces of paper—one yellow orange and one pale nude. You could use scissors for the outer edges if you prefer.

**2.** Use an embossing tool and ruler to score the score lines on all the pieces. Use a bone folder to crease along each score line to make valleys.

**3.** Layer up each flower with a large petal piece, small petal piece, and stamen piece. Apply a thin layer of tacky glue to the back of each small petal piece, then attach to the corresponding large petal piece, aligning the creases. There should be one empty large petal segment once glued. Apply a dot of glue to the center of the stamen piece and attach it to the center of the petal piece, positioning it so that two stamens are on each small petal.

### Tip
Make your scored lines and creases as accurate as you can to make the paper work as smoothly as possible.

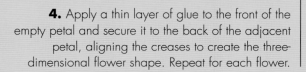

**4.** Apply a thin layer of glue to the front of the empty petal and secure it to the back of the adjacent petal, aligning the creases to create the three-dimensional flower shape. Repeat for each flower.

**5.** Flatten each flower and arrange in the positions shown, ready to assemble the pop-up.

**6.** Work from left to right, beginning with the blush flower: position the flattened flower with petals pointing toward the left and apply a line of glue along the curved tip of the top petal. Take the yellow top-left flower and rotate it so that the petal tips are facing away from you. Press the yellow flower onto the blush flower, aligning the left yellow petal with the top blush petal. Apply a line of glue along the curved tip of the bottom blush petal. Take the yellow bottom-left flower and rotate it so that the petal tips are facing toward you. Place the yellow flower onto the blush flower, aligning the left yellow petal with the bottom blush petal as shown.

**7.** Take the pink central flower and apply a line of glue along the curved tips of the three visible petals as shown.

**8.** Turn the pink flower over and press it onto the previously glued flowers, aligning the pink central petal with the blush central petal, and the pink top and bottom petals with the yellow petals beneath. Apply a line of glue along the curved tip of the top and bottom pink petals.

**9.** Repeat the technique of Steps 6–8, rotating the next two flowers and aligning with the petals beneath, pressing to secure. Apply a line of glue along the curved tips of the three left-facing petals as shown.

**10.** Place the final yellow flower on top, aligning with the petals beneath and pressing to secure. Fold each outer piece in half, then unfold.

**11.** Stack up the outer layers, with blush pink on the top, followed by pastel yellow, yellow orange, then pale nude. Check that they are all aligned properly by looking at the cut-out flower design. Glue the layers together with a line of glue between each piece as shown.

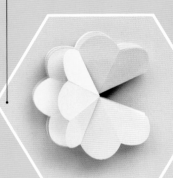

**12.** Fold the glued stack of paper in half along the line creased in Step 2, then trim the edges using the metal ruler, X-acto knife, and cutting mat; then unfold.

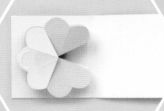

### Customize it
Cut out leaf shapes and glue around the flowers, or experiment with different-shaped petal tips.

**13.** Take the glued flowers and apply a line of glue along the curved tip of the central petal on each face of the stack. Position inside the layered card outer piece, with the petals facing away from the crease of the card outer piece, and a gap of 1/5 – 2/5 in. (5–10 mm) between the flower stack and the card outer crease.

**14.** Close the card and gently press while the glue begins to dry. Once dry, open and close your card.

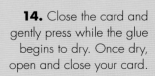

# 15

# GEOMETRIC POT WRAP

This geometric plant-pot wrap is a great project for practicing cutting straight lines with an X-acto knife. The template is sized to fit a plant pot with a width of 2¾ in. (7 cm) and height of 2¼ in. (5.5 cm), but it can easily be scaled to fit any size of pot. Try different shapes, such as half-cut circles, to create a different pattern.

## YOU WILL NEED

**1** 8¼ × 11¾ in. (A4) sheet of paper in blush pink   **2** 8¼ × 11¾ in. (A4) sheet of card in dark pink
**3** Small painting roller and tray
**4** Dark red paint   **5** X-acto knife   **6** Cutting mat   **7** Metal ruler   **8** Bone folder
**9** All-purpose adhesive
**10** Plant pot with a solid base

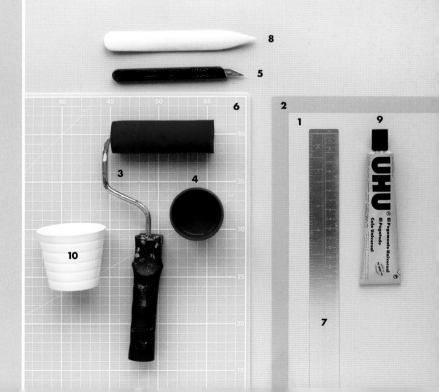

# TO MAKE

**1.** Use a roller to evenly paint one side of the blush-pink paper with dark red paint. Apply the paint in thin coats, allowing it to dry between each one, until fully covered.

**2.** Using the corresponding template (see page 140), cut out the the main piece and make the half-cuts as shown, using an X-acto knife, cutting mat, and metal ruler.

**3.** Fold each triangle-shaped half-cut back on itself and flatten the crease with a bone folder.

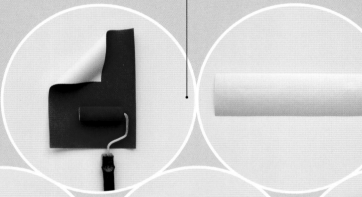

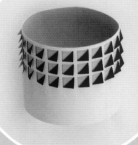

**4.** Cut a rectangle of dark pink card measuring 8½ × 2⅖ in. (22 × 6 cm).

**5.** Apply a line of all-purpose adhesive down the back of the left-hand edge of the blush-pink piece, then position on top of the dark pink piece, aligning the edges.

**6.** Glue the right-hand edge of the two layers together, then immediately (while the glue is still wet) apply a line of adhesive down the front right edge of the blush piece. Gently roll the strip into a ring as shown, and press the glued line onto the back of the other end.

# 16

# ORIGAMI LAMPSHADE

Strictly speaking, this lampshade isn't origami, but it's a great project to put your paper-folding skills to the test. Once you break the folding down into a step of valley folds followed by a step of mountain folds, it is fairly straightforward, and when mastered, you will be making bespoke lampshades for every room in the house!

## YOU WILL NEED

**1** 3 11¾ × 16½ in. (A3) sheets of
light card in marble
**2** Cutting mat   **3** Metal ruler
**4** Embossing tool   **5** Bone folder   **6** Pencil
**7** Eraser   **8** Scissors   **9** Tacky glue
**10** Stapler   **11** Self-adhesive Velcro pads
**12** Ceiling light fitting
* LED light bulb (not pictured)

**Warning**
For safety, make sure you only
use an LED light bulb.

# TO MAKE

**1.** Place the first sheet of marble card in a landscape position on a cutting mat. Use a ruler and embossing tool to score a vertical line ⅖ in. (1 cm) from the right edge.

**2.** Measure and score seven equally spaced vertical lines to divide the space between the left side of the paper and the line scored in Step 1 into eight equal sections. Use a bone folder to fold each scored line to make a valley fold, then unfold.

**3.** Measure 8½ in. (22 cm) from the top of the first, third, fifth, and seventh fold, and make a small pencil mark. Use a ruler and embossing tool to score lines joining each pencil mark to the top and bottom of the fold lines on either side. Rub out the pencil marks.

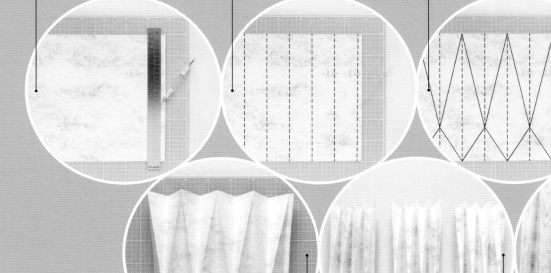

**4.** Fold each scored line from Step 3 into a mountain fold. The paper should now form the shape shown (it may need a little encouragement).

**5.** Repeat Steps 1–4 for the remaining two sheets of card.

**6.** Use scissors to cut off the top and bottom corners of the ⅖ in. (1 cm) strip on the right of each piece to make a tab. The corners should be cut at a reflection of the angle of the adjacent folded line as shown.

**7.** Flatten each piece and turn to the side. Use scissors to make a cut through all layers in the position shown, beginning around 1⅕ in. (3 cm) down from the end of the fold and finishing at the top point.

**8.** Glue the three pieces together: apply a thin layer of tacky glue to the front of the tab, down the right side of the first piece, and attach it behind the left edge of the next piece, aligning along the top and bottom edges.

**9.** Cut along the second mountain fold from the right end as shown. Discard the small piece.

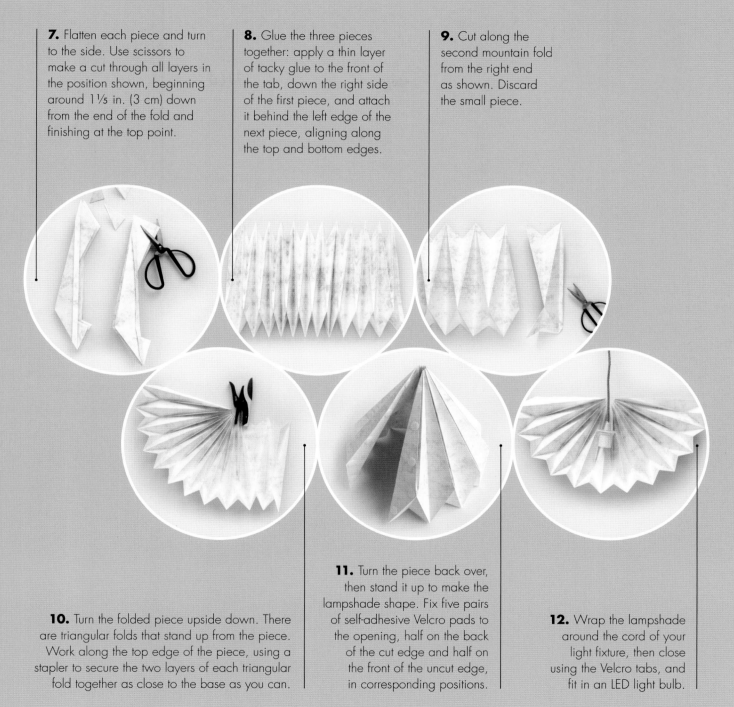

**10.** Turn the folded piece upside down. There are triangular folds that stand up from the piece. Work along the top edge of the piece, using a stapler to secure the two layers of each triangular fold together as close to the base as you can.

**11.** Turn the piece back over, then stand it up to make the lampshade shape. Fix five pairs of self-adhesive Velcro pads to the opening, half on the back of the cut edge and half on the front of the uncut edge, in corresponding positions.

**12.** Wrap the lampshade around the cord of your light fixture, then close using the Velcro tabs, and fit in an LED light bulb.

# 17

# GEM GARLAND

Not only is this "gem" of a garland perfect for celebrations, but it can also add a pop of color and graphic style to your home all year round. I opted for jewel tones, but you could make the garland in your wedding colors to add some fun to the decor on your big day, or use a festive palette and string the garland around your Christmas tree or along your mantelpiece.

## YOU WILL NEED

8¼ × 11¾ in. (A4) sheet of paper in:
**1** mint  **2** dark red  **3** teal  **4** blush pink
**5** 8¼ × 11¾ in. (A4) sheet of metallic paper in copper  **6** 8¼ × 11¾ in. (A4) sheet of paper in pearlescent rose gold
**7** X-acto knife  **8** Cutting mat  **9** Scissors
**10** Embossing tool  **11** Metal ruler
* Bone folder (not pictured)  **12** Tacky glue
**13** Tapestry needle  **14** Crimp beads
**15** Fishing wire, 67 in. (170 cm)
**16** Flat-nose pliers

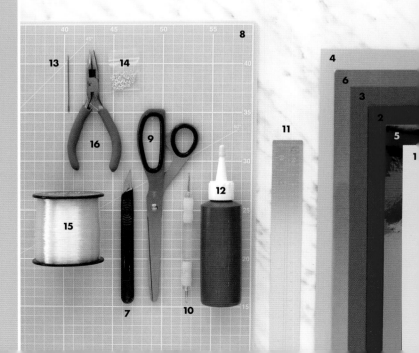

# TO MAKE

**2.** Use an embossing tool and ruler to score the fold lines. Use a bone folder to crease each score line into a mountain fold.

**3.** Each template has one face with no tabs, which is labeled on the template. Each shape needs to be partially assembled, leaving the tab-less face unglued. To do this, work around the shape, gluing each tab to the back of the adjacent side, unless the adjacent side is on the tab-less face. If it is, leave the tab unglued. This should leave the shape assembled aside from the tab-less face, which should hinge open.

**1.** Use the corresponding templates (see page 127) to cut out the three shapes in your choice of color combinations, using an X-acto knife and a cutting mat, or scissors if you prefer.

**4.** Use a tapestry needle to pierce a hole through one point of the shape, at the opposite end of the shape to one of the points of the hinged side.

**5.** Thread a crimp bead onto the fishing wire and hold it 10 in. (25 cm) from one end of the wire. Use flat-nose pliers to squeeze it closed. After fixing a crimp in place, it can be handy to give it a little pull with your fingers to check that it is secure.

**6.** Take your first shape. Thread the long end of the wire in through the pierced hole, and pull the wire out through the hinged face. Position the shape so that the wire enters the pieced hole and exits through the opposite point of the shape.

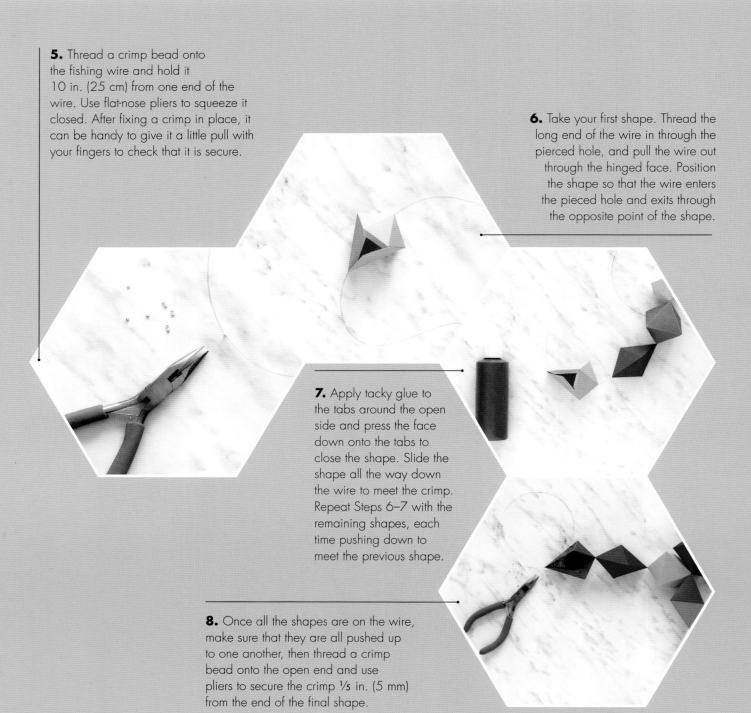

**7.** Apply tacky glue to the tabs around the open side and press the face down onto the tabs to close the shape. Slide the shape all the way down the wire to meet the crimp. Repeat Steps 6–7 with the remaining shapes, each time pushing down to meet the previous shape.

**8.** Once all the shapes are on the wire, make sure that they are all pushed up to one another, then thread a crimp bead onto the open end and use pliers to secure the crimp ⅕ in. (5 mm) from the end of the final shape.

# 18

# PAPER PLANT

Sometimes, despite our best efforts, keeping a houseplant alive and flourishing can be a challenge. If, like me, you sometimes have a bit of a black thumb, fake a little greenery in your home with this no-maintenance paper plant. It is a version of a variegated prayer plant I had, which I loved—and actually managed to keep alive—but sadly had to be adopted by a friend when I moved.

## YOU WILL NEED

2 8¼ × 11¾ in. (A4) sheets of paper in:
**1** green **2** pink **3** 8¼ × 11¾ in. (A4) sheet of light card in marble
**4** 5¾ × 8¼ in. (A5) sheet of paper in tan
**5** X-acto knife **6** Cutting mat **7** Scissors
**8** Embossing tool **9** Metal ruler
**10** Bone folder **11** Paintbrush
**12** Pale-pink acrylic paint **13** Thick pen (or other similar-sized cylinder)
**14** 12 green floral wires, 12 in. (30 cm)
**15** Tacky glue **16** Pliers with wire cutters
**17** Floral tape **18** Pair of compasses
**19** Double-sided self-adhesive foam

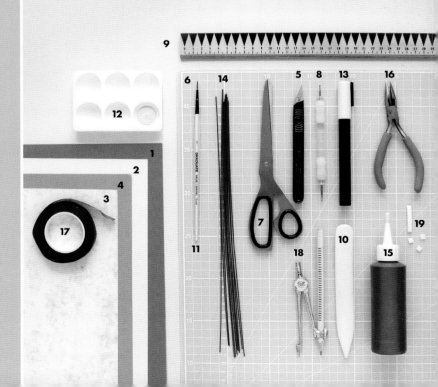

# TO MAKE

**1.** Using the corresponding templates (see page 133), cut out each piece with an X-acto knife and a cutting mat, or scissors if you prefer.

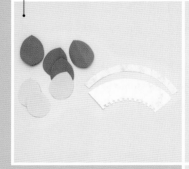

**2.** Use an embossing tool and ruler to score the fold lines. Use a bone folder to crease along each scored line to create a valley fold.

**3.** Using small brushstrokes, paint the pale-pink pattern onto the green leaves, building up the pattern as shown, then allow to dry.

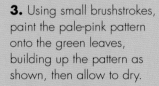

**4.** One at a time, take a leaf and roll each side of it (parallel to the fold) around a thick pen to curl the edges of the leaf backward. Repeat for all leaves, both pink and green.

**5.** Take the first wire and apply a line of tacky glue down from one end to ⅘ in. (2 cm). Attach to a pink leaf, placing on top of the valley fold, so that the wire covers about ⅘ in. (2 cm) of the fold at the base (wider end) of the leaf. Repeat for all remaining pink leaves.

**6.** Take a painted leaf and apply a thin layer of glue all over the back. Place it on top of a pink leaf so that the wire is sandwiched between the two layers with edges aligned. Repeat for all remaining leaves.

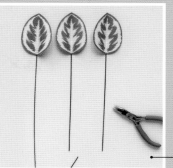

**7.** Separate three stemmed leaves from the other nine. Use pliers with wire cutters to trim the wire so the stems measure 7½ in. (19 cm) each.

**8.** Separate six stemmed leaves from the remaining nine, and trim the wire so the stems measure 6 in. (15 cm) each. This should leave you with three full-length wires, three 7½ in. (19 cm) wires, and six 6 in. (15 cm) wires.

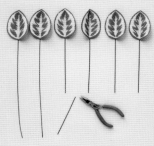

**10.** Take the three medium-stemmed leaves. Again, make a 3 in. (8 cm) curve in each wire, starting just below the leaf. Hold the stems around the wires bound in Step 9, one between each, but with the ends at the bottom of the tape-wrapped area rather than overhanging. Use floral tape to wrap the wires over the top of the area that was wrapped in Step 9.

**9.** Take the three longest-stemmed leaves. Use your fingers to make a gentle curve in the wire along a length of 3 in. (8 cm), starting just below the leaf. Then use floral tape to wrap the three wires together, starting 3 in. (8 cm) from the bottom of the wires and stopping 1 in. (2.5 cm) from the bottom. Use pliers to bend the bottom wire ends just below the tape to right angles, pointing outward in different directions.

**11.** Repeat with the six remaining leaves, making a 3 in. (8 cm) curve in each wire just below the leaf. Then, holding the stems around the bound wires, use floral tape to wrap over the top of the existing taped area.

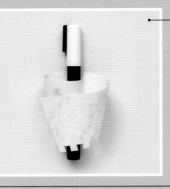

**12.** Use a pair of compasses to draw out two 2 in. (5 cm) circles onto the marble card, and cut them out.

**13.** Roll the large marble plant pot piece around the thick pen and release to create a slight curl.

**14.** Fold each of the little square tabs to a right angle into the curl, then turn the piece so that the end with the tabs is pointing upward. Apply glue to the inside of the first tab and attach it to a circle piece as shown, so that the tab is on top of the circle. Hold this tab in place while the glue dries.

**15.** Apply glue to the inside of the remaining tabs, as well as a line of glue along the inside of the loose end's straight-sided edge. Working quickly, before the glue dries, and starting from the first glued tab, press each tab onto the circle, trying to avoid creating gaps between the two pieces. When you have worked all the way around, overlap the ends, securing in place with the preglued edge. Note that due to the nature of the shape, the overlap will naturally be slightly greater at the open end of the pot than the base.

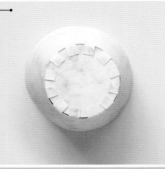

**16.** Apply a thin layer of glue to the back of the second circle piece and press onto the bottom of the pot to cover the glued tabs.

**17.** Cut ten squares of double-sided self-adhesive foam, ⅕ × ⅕ in. (5 × 5 mm) each, and fix at regular intervals around the outside of the top edge of the pot, touching the edge.

**18.** Wrap the curved strip of marble card around the top of the pot, aligning the bottom edge of the strip with the bottom edge of the foam pads, pressing over each pad to secure. When you get all the way around, apply glue to the overlapping section and attach in place.

**19.** Take your tan paper. Use the pair of compasses to draw a 3 in. (8 cm) circle in the paper with a ⅕ in. (5 mm) circle in its center. Cut out both circles.

**20.** Take the bound wire stem and straighten out the three bent wire ends. Thread the stem through the hole in the tan circle, then use pliers to rebend each of the three long wires back to a right angle.

**21.** Apply glue to the inside of the plant pot base, as well as around the underside edge of the tan circle. Place the plant in the pot, pushing the wires down to encourage them to adhere to the base, as well as applying pressure around the edge of the tan circle.

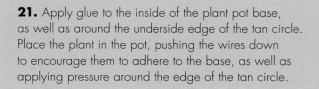

# 19

# CACTUS DESK TIDY

I love cacti, partly because I can keep them alive but mostly for their form, repetition, and beautiful, naturally geometric shapes. This little paper cactus is the perfect accessory to add some greenery to your desk— it even doubles as a storage box.

## YOU WILL NEED

**1** 2 8¼ × 11¾ in. (A4) sheets of card in gold   **2** 8¼ × 11¾ in. (A4) sheet of paper in green
**3** 5¾ × 8¼ in. (A5) sheet of card in blush pink   **4** 8¼ × 11¾ in. (A4) sheet of card in pink
**5** X-acto knife   **6** Cutting mat   **7** Scissors
**8** Embossing tool   **9** Metal ruler
**10** Bone folder   **11** Pencil   **12** Tacky glue
**13** Split pin    * Hole punch (not pictured)
**14** Pliers   **15** Wooden skewer

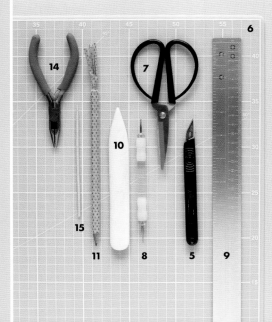

# TO MAKE

**1.** Using the corresponding templates (see pages 138–139), cut out each piece as shown using an X-acto knife and a cutting mat, or scissors if you prefer.

**2.** Use an embossing tool and ruler to score the fold lines. Use a bone folder to crease along each score line to make a mountain fold. Also crease the spikes on the cactus piece upward.

**3.** Cut out a strip of gold card measuring 8¼ × ¾ in. (21 × 2 cm). Measure out and score six evenly spaced vertical lines to divide the strip into seven equal sections. There should be a gap of 1³⁄₁₆ in. (3 cm) between each scored line. Fold along each scored line.

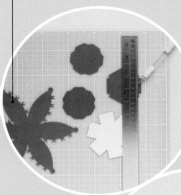

**4.** Take the large pink piece and position with the hexagon section flat on the table and the rectangles folded to point upward at a right angle. Apply tacky glue to the back of the gold strip and wrap around the vertically folded sides of the pink piece. Overlap the end sections of the gold strip, gluing one on top of the other.

**5.** Cut an 8¼ × 3 in. (21 × 8 cm) rectangle of gold card, then measure out and score six evenly spaced vertical lines, 1³⁄₁₆ in. (3 cm) apart. Cut an 8 × 3 in. (20.3 × 8 cm) rectangle of pink card, then measure out and score six evenly spaced vertical lines, 1⅛ in. (2.9 cm) apart. Fold along each scored line.

**6.** Apply a thin layer of tacky glue to the back of one end section of the pink rectangle, then overlap it with the section at the opposite end, aligning the edges. Take one of the gold hexagon pieces with angled tabs. Apply glue to the inside of each tab and attach to one end of the pink hexagonal tube, positioning one tab on the outside of each face of the tube.

**7.** Take the gold rectangle cut in Step 5, apply a thin layer of glue all over the back, and wrap around the pink hexagonal tube, overlapping the end sections of the gold rectangle and aligning the edges.

### Preparation

Try to be as accurate as you can when measuring the rectangles. Measure each length at several points, marking accurately with a sharp pencil, then join together using a ruler.

**8.** Cut an 8¼ × 1¾ in. (21 × 4.5 cm) rectangle of gold card, then measure out and score six evenly spaced vertical lines, 1³⁄₁₆ in. (3 cm) apart. Cut another rectangle of gold card measuring 8¹³⁄₁₆ × 2¼ in. (22.4 × 6 cm), then measure out and score six evenly spaced vertical lines, 1¼ in. (3.2 cm) apart. Fold along each scored line.

**9.** Take the smaller rectangle cut in Step 8 and the remaining gold hexagon piece with angled tabs. This time, apply glue to the outside of the tabs and wrap the rectangle around it, attaching one tab to the inside bottom edge of each face. Overlap and glue the end sections of the gold rectangle, aligning the edges.

**10.** Take the remaining rectangle from Step 8 and the gold hexagon piece with rectangular tabs. Apply glue to the outside of the tabs and position so that the end edge of each tab is aligned with the top edge of the rectangle. Wrap the rectangle around, making sure to keep each tab aligned with the top, then overlap and glue the end sections.

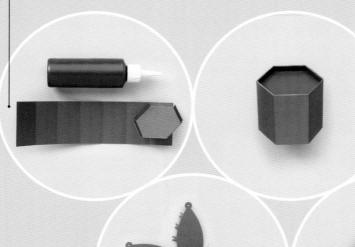

### Hone your skills
It can get fussy trying to thread the sections onto the split pin, but I find that it helps to grip the split pin legs with pliers—they are smaller than fingers, so you can still see what you are doing.

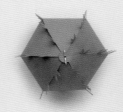

**11.** Turn the green piece upside down so that the mountain folds are now valley folds. Use a hole punch to punch small holes in each of the six small circles. Curve one section of the piece upward and back on itself, then push a split pin through the small hole from bottom to top. The second piece to curve up is the section adjacent to the smooth edge of the first piece, not the spiked side. Work around the piece in this direction, curving each section up and over and adding onto the split pin. It can help to grip the end of the split pin with pliers.

**12.** To add the final section, grip the top of the split pin and push it, along with the paper layers, downward, to create a gap between each face of the cactus. Carefully, put your finger into one of the gaps, push the bottom of the split pin upward, then open out and flatten its legs on top.

**13.** Apply a thin layer of glue to the base of the cactus piece, then press it centrally onto the top of the gold piece glued in Step 10.

**14.** Take the flower pieces and roll each petal around a wooden skewer. Glue the flowers one on top of another, positioning the petals of each layer in between the petals of the previous layer. Arrange with the two larger flowers on the bottom and two smaller flowers on top. Glue onto the top of the cactus, covering the split pin legs.

**15.** Place the cactus lid over the gold base glued in Step 10 to make a storage box. Arrange alongside the tall pen pot and small trinket tray.

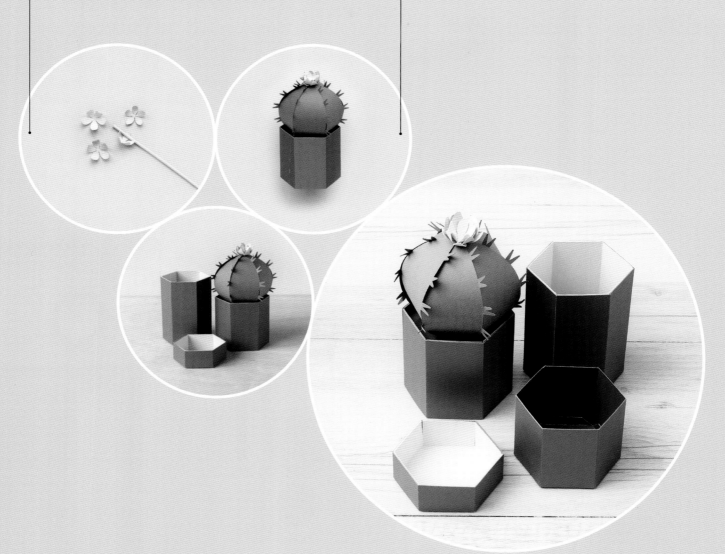

# 20
# GIANT POPPY

Seeing poppies begin to bloom in spring is one of my favorite sights. The grand scale of this flower is especially striking, and I chose crepe paper to mimic the delicate, crinkled texture of the petals.

## YOU WILL NEED

**1** 11¾ × 16½ in. (A3) sheet of light card in green  **2** 11¾ × 16½ in. (A3) sheet of paper in black  **3** Roll of heavyweight crepe paper in pink  **4** Roll of lightweight crepe paper in black
**5** X-acto knife  **6** Cutting mat  **7** Scissors
**8** Embossing tool  **9** Metal ruler
**10** Tacky glue  **11** 3 green floral wires, 12 in. (30 cm)  **12** Black acrylic paint
**13** Paintbrush  **14** Polystyrene ball, 2⅓ in. (6 cm) diameter  **15** Wooden dowel, 1 in. (25 mm) diameter  **16** Hot glue gun
**17** Green floral tape

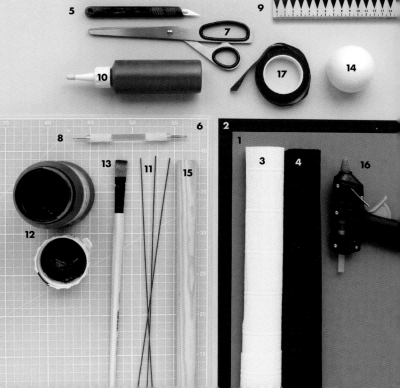

# TO MAKE

**1.** Using the corresponding templates (see pages 142–143), cut out three leaf shapes and two stamen shapes using an X-acto knife and a cutting mat, or scissors if you prefer.

**2.** Use an embossing tool and ruler to score the fold lines. Fold each scored line into a valley fold by turning the leaves over and making mountain folds on the back. Fold down the center first, then unfold. For the curved creases, use the side of one finger to push from behind and the other hand to gently squeeze either side of each leaf to form a mountain fold. Repeat with every scored line, then turn the leaves back the right way up so that the folds are valley folds.

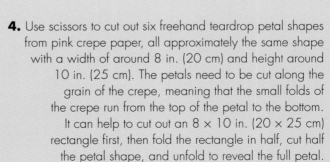

**3.** Apply a line of tacky glue down the center of each leaf, then press a length of floral wire onto the glue, aligning the end of the wire with the top point of the leaf. Leave to dry, then make a bend in the floral wire (and the paper leaf) where shown.

**4.** Use scissors to cut out six freehand teardrop petal shapes from pink crepe paper, all approximately the same shape with a width of around 8 in. (20 cm) and height around 10 in. (25 cm). The petals need to be cut along the grain of the crepe, meaning that the small folds of the crepe run from the top of the petal to the bottom. It can help to cut out an 8 × 10 in. (20 × 25 cm) rectangle first, then fold the rectangle in half, cut half the petal shape, and unfold to reveal the full petal.

**5.** Paint the marking shown onto each petal using acrylic paint in sweeping brushstrokes. If the crepe paper gets too wet, it stretches out of shape, so try to keep it as dry as possible, using only a small amount of paint on your brush and building it up in layers. Leave to dry.

**6.** Stretch the crepe slightly in the center and along the top edge of each petal: hold the petal with your thumbs in the center where you applied the paint, and gently pull the paper out to the sides to cup the petal. Work along the top edge of the petal, making little sideways pulls with your fingers to gently stretch the crepe and create a wavy top edge.

### Variation
Try using different-colored crepe papers to make a striking red poppy or elegant white anemone.

**7.** Use the X-acto knife to trim a little slice away from the polystyrene ball. This flat face is the bottom of the ball. Cut a piece of black crepe paper large enough to wrap around the polystyrene ball, then apply dots of tacky glue to the crepe paper and stretch it around the ball so that the excess crepe paper gathers on the bottom.

**8.** Take the wooden dowel, two black stamen pieces, and the paper-covered ball. Bend each stamen up from the center circle, then use tacky glue to attach one stamen piece on top of the other, aligning so that the stamens of the top layer are positioned in between the stamens of the bottom layer. Use a glue gun to attach the polystyrene ball to the center of the stamen pieces, then use the glue gun to attach the whole thing to the top of the wooden dowel.

**9.** Hold the dowel upside down. Take the first three petals and use the glue gun to apply glue to the base of each petal. Attach to the wooden dowel, evenly spaced around the stamens.

**10.** Repeat Step 9 with the remaining three petals, attaching each petal between the previously glued petals. This time, once the petals are attached at the base, glue the sides of the petals to the backs of the petals glued in Step 9 to create a sturdier flower shape and prevent the petals from flopping down.

**11.** Wrap the top 4 in. (10 cm) of the wooden dowel with floral tape, stretching the tape as you wrap.

### Display idea
Repeat the flower heads without the stems to create a stunning floral backdrop wall.

**12.** Use the glue gun to attach the three leaves to the wooden dowel around the bottom of the taped section, arranging them at slightly differing heights. Continue to wrap the dowel with floral tape, wrapping over the bases of the leaves and all the way to the bottom of the dowel.

# 21
# FLORAL GARLAND

To me, a home without flowers is not a home at all. But fresh flowers are so expensive and only last a few days, so this bright floral garland is the perfect way to add the color and beauty of flowers to your home every day.

## YOU WILL NEED

$5\frac{3}{4} \times 8\frac{1}{4}$ in. (A5) sheet of paper in: **1** dark yellow
**2** orange  **3** blush pink  **4** yellow
**5** 2 $8\frac{1}{4} \times 11\frac{3}{4}$ in. (A4) sheets of paper in green
**6** X-acto knife  **7** Cutting mat
**8** Scissors  **9** Embossing tool
**10** Metal ruler  **11** Tacky glue
**12** Grosgrain ribbon, 40 in. (1 m)
**13** Hot glue gun

# TO MAKE

**1.** Using the corresponding templates (see page 140), cut out each piece as shown, using an X-acto knife and a cutting mat, or scissors if you prefer.

**2.** Use an embossing tool and ruler to score the fold lines. Fold each scored line into a valley fold by turning the leaves over and making mountain folds on the back. Work around the leaves one at a time. Use the side of one finger to push from behind and the other hand to gently squeeze either side of each leaf to form the mountain fold. Repeat with every leaf, then put the folded leaves to one side.

**3.** Take the green stem pieces, colored bud pieces, and smaller flower pieces. On the stem pieces, apply a small amount of tacky glue along the front edge of each of the V-shaped ends, then press two buds and a flower onto the glue in the positions shown. Take a second stem piece and apply a thin layer of glue all over the back, then press the stem onto the previously glued pieces so that the buds and flower are sandwiched between the two green layers as shown. Align the edges before the glue dries.

**4.** Cut two 1½ × 1½ in. (4 × 4 cm) squares in each color except green, then use scissors to fringe along one edge, making cuts close together and cutting down to around ¼ in. (7 mm) from the end.

**5.** Take the fringed pieces and ribbon. Use a glue gun to apply a line of hot glue along the base of the first fringed piece before wrapping it tightly around the ribbon, approximately 8 in. (20 cm) from one end. Repeat with the other fringed pieces, positioning along the ribbon with a gap of around 3½ in. (9 cm) between the end of one fringe and the beginning of the next.

**6.** Attach the large flower pieces to the garland: take the first flower piece and apply a thin layer of tacky glue to the front of the end petal and a line of glue around the base of the first fringe. Wrap the flower around the ribbon below the fringe, overlap the two end petals, align the edges, and press together while the glue dries, pushing the flower up into the glue around the fringe.

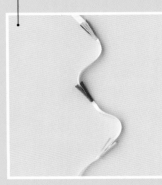

### Customize it
Choose a ribbon to match your wall color, and let the flowers take the spotlight.

### Variations
For a simpler garland, you could just use the large flowers with fringed centers.

The large flower template can be used to make stemmed flowers too—just make the fringed center and wrap around the end of a piece of floral wire, then glue the flower piece below it, and bind the wire with floral tape, adding leaves if you wish.

**7.** Take the large leaves and the stems. Use the hot glue gun to fix the end of each piece to the ribbon, attaching at angles as shown and arranging so that one leaf piece and one stem piece are positioned between each flower.

**8.** Use the hot glue gun to attach the small leaf pieces to the garland, positioning to cover the end of each leaf and stem piece.

# 22

# PAJAKI PAPER CHANDELIER

This project was inspired by *pajaki*, a colorful, Polish folk art designed to resemble crystal chandeliers. *Pajaki*, which translates literally as "spiders of straw," were traditionally made using reeds, paper, yarn, and ribbon, and were used to brighten up the home during winter. My interpretation of these vibrant decorations is made from a mixture of paper garlands, honeycomb balls, and tissue tassels, and it's perfect as a party centerpiece or to add a pop of color to your home all year round.

## YOU WILL NEED

**1** 7 8¼ × 11¾ in. (A4) sheets of paper in navy blue
**2** 5¾ × 8¼ in. (A5) sheet of grayboard
2 8¼ × 11¾ in. (A4) sheets of paper in:
**3** bright blue  **4** blush pink
Sheet of tissue paper in: * blue   * blush pink
(not pictured)  **5** 12 in. (30.5 cm) wooden embroidery
hoop (inside ring only)  **6** Navy blue paint
**7** Paintbrush  **8** Scrap paper  **9** Pencil
**10** Scissors  **11** X-acto knife  **12** Cutting mat
**13** Metal ruler  **14** Bone folder  **15** Hot glue gun
**16** Sewing machine  **17** Bright blue thread
**18** Blush-pink thread  **19** Gold washi tape
**20** 8 2 in. (5 cm) blue-paper honeycomb balls

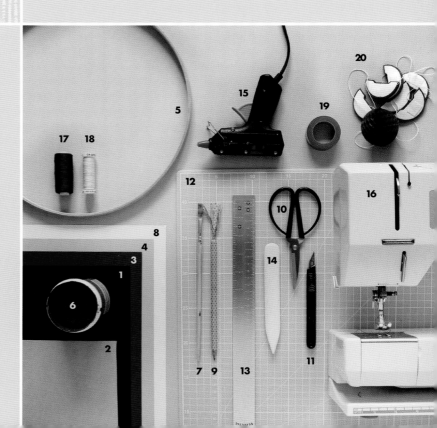

**1.** Paint the embroidery hoop with navy blue paint and allow to dry. Draw around the hoop onto scrap paper and cut out. Fold the paper circle in half, then quarters, then eighths, and then unfold it.

**2.** Place the paper circle below the hoop, then make eight pencil marks on the hoop, using the positions of the paper folds as a guide.

**3.** Using the corresponding templates (see page 139), cut out 80 navy blue pieces and the grayboard octagon using an X-acto knife, cutting mat, and metal ruler, or scissors if you prefer. Paint the octagon navy blue and allow to dry.

**4.** Use a bone folder to fold all 80 navy blue pieces in half, creasing across the narrow section. Sandwich one folded navy piece around each side of the octagon ring, with the crease on the inner edge of the octagon. To fit the back half of each piece through the center of the octagon, gently squeeze the sides of the back half of the paper piece together, creating a slight fold to make the piece fit the gap, then push through the center of the octagon and flatten back out.

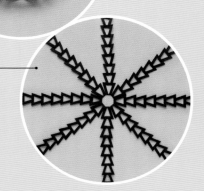

**5.** Link the navy pieces to one another to make chains, beginning with the pieces attached to the octagon in Step 4. To link the pieces, repeat the process used to sandwich the pieces around the octagon in Step 4, but thread the back layer of each piece through the center of the previous piece, sandwiching around both layers of the bottom of the previous piece. Repeat until each chain has ten pieces in total.

**6.** The end piece of each chain should have an open end. Use a glue gun to attach each of these open ends to the painted embroidery hoop, one layer on the outside of the hoop and one on the inside, positioning over the pencil marks made in Step 2.

**7.** Use the ruler, X-acto knife, and cutting mat to cut 24 ⅖ in. (1 cm) strips from the long edge of the bright blue paper. Cut each strip into five equally sized pieces.

**8.** Use a sewing machine to stitch the strips together in eight groups of 15. Stitch a line of bright blue thread around ⅕ in. (5 mm) from the top of the first piece, then stitch straight onto the second piece, leaving no gap between the pieces and aligning the edges. Once you have attached the first 15 pieces together, cut the thread and begin the next group of 15, repeating the process.

**9.** Use the glue gun to attach the top of each stitched strip to the hoop, in the positions shown.

**10.** Cut 72 1 in. (2.5 cm) squares of blush-pink paper. Use the sewing machine to stitch the squares together in eight groups of nine. Stitch a line of blush-pink thread diagonally though each square, leaving no gap between the pieces. Once you have attached the first nine pieces together, cut the thread and begin the next group of nine, repeating the process.

**11.** Cut eight 9 × 6¾ in. (23 × 17 cm) pieces of blue tissue paper. Fold each one in half lengthwise, then use the metal ruler, X-acto knife, and cutting mat to fringe the tissue, cutting vertical lines a fraction of an inch apart, each time stopping ⅖ in. (1 cm) from the folded edge.

**12.** Unfold each fringed sheet, then roll and twist up the middle section. Fold the twisted piece in half, then wrap the twisted section with gold washi tape. Repeat for each piece, making eight tassels.

**13.** Use the glue gun to attach one tassel to the back of the central piece on each pink-stitched strip in the position shown. Use the glue gun to attach each end-stitched piece to the hoop in the positions shown.

**Variation**
Try making tissue-paper pom-poms instead of using honeycomb balls.

**14.** Repeat Steps 11 and 12 using blush-pink tissue paper to make eight pink tissue tassels.

**15.** Take the honeycomb balls and pink tassels. Half open the first ball, then use the glue gun to attach a pink tassel to the back. Use the glue gun to apply hot glue to the two cardboard faces of the tissue ball and attach to the hoop in the position shown. Repeat for all balls and tassels.

to:

return address:

## 23

# CUCKOO CLOCK

This modern, fun cuckoo clock, which still retains a touch of Bavarian kitsch, is one of my favorite projects in this book. It definitely requires a little patience to make, but the end result is utterly adorable and undoubtedly impressive, sure to make a statement on your wall.

## YOU WILL NEED

5¾ × 8¼ in. (A5) sheet of paper in:
**1** peach   **2** coral
**3** 5¾ × 8¼ in. (A5) sheet of single-sided mirror paper in gold
**4** 2 8¼ × 11¾ in. (A4) sheets of paper in pale peach   **5** 11¾ × 16½ in. (A3) sheet of paper in navy
**6** X-acto knife   **7** Cutting mat   **8** Metal ruler
**9** Scissors   **10** Embossing tool
**11** Bone folder   **12** Tacky glue
**13** Pair of compasses   **14** Clock mechanism
**15** Double-sided self-adhesive foam pads

# TO MAKE

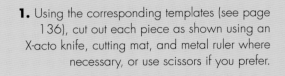

**1.** Using the corresponding templates (see page 136), cut out each piece as shown using an X-acto knife, cutting mat, and metal ruler where necessary, or use scissors if you prefer.

**2.** Use an embossing tool and ruler to score the fold lines. Use a bone folder to fold each score line into a mountain or valley according to the template labels.

**3.** Take the large navy piece. Apply a thin layer of tacky glue to the back of the side tab and attach it to the back of the opposite edge of the piece.

**4.** One face at a time, close the roof and the base of the large navy piece. To do this, apply a thin layer of glue to each tab around the first open face, then lower the hinged face down onto the glued tabs and press while the glue begins to dry. Repeat this with all remaining hinged sides to complete the house shape.

**5.** Separate the pale peach scalloped pieces into those with the creases between two scallops and those with the creases through a scallop. Begin with a piece where the creases are between two scallops, and apply a line of glue along the back of the top straight edge. Attach it to the navy house piece, wrapping around the sides and positioning it so that the bottom of the scallops align with the bottom edge of the house.

**6.** Repeat Step 5 with the remaining scalloped pieces, alternating between the two types of piece, and each time aligning the bottom of the scallops with the tops of the cuts in between the scallops on the previously glued strip.

**7.** Turn the scalloped house over, place on a cutting mat, and use the X-acto knife to cut through the scalloped strips where the hole in the navy piece is so that there is now once again a hole all the way through the front of the house.

**8.** Apply a thin layer of glue to the back of the triangular peach piece. Attach to the navy house, aligning the angled edges with the roof of the house and aligning the window hole.

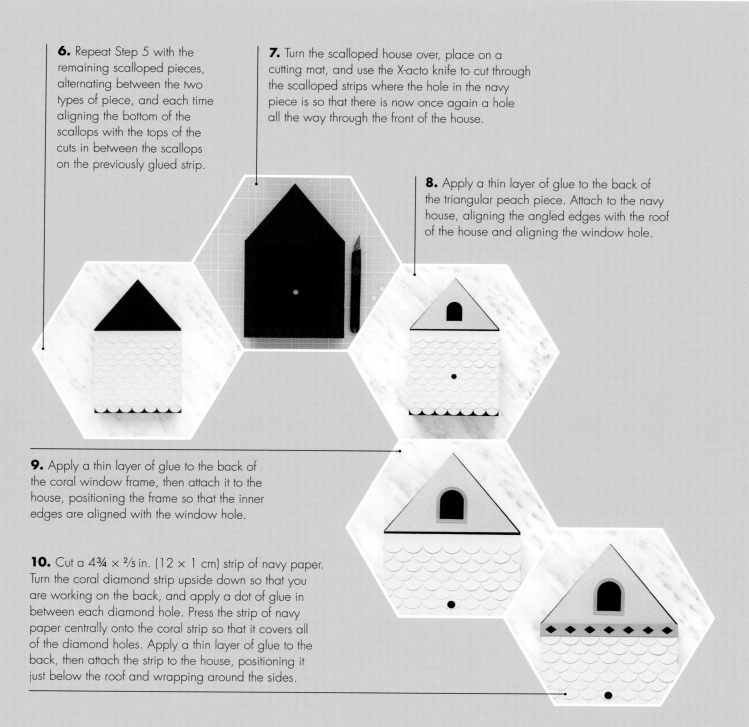

**9.** Apply a thin layer of glue to the back of the coral window frame, then attach it to the house, positioning the frame so that the inner edges are aligned with the window hole.

**10.** Cut a 4¾ × ⅖ in. (12 × 1 cm) strip of navy paper. Turn the coral diamond strip upside down so that you are working on the back, and apply a dot of glue in between each diamond hole. Press the strip of navy paper centrally onto the coral strip so that it covers all of the diamond holes. Apply a thin layer of glue to the back, then attach the strip to the house, positioning it just below the roof and wrapping around the sides.

**11.** Use a pair of compasses to draw three circles: one on gold paper with a 2¾ in. (7 cm) diameter; one on coral paper with a 2½ in. (6.5 cm) diameter; and one on peach paper with a 1¾ in. (4.5 cm) diameter. In the center of each circle, draw another circle, with a diameter of ¼ in. (7 mm). Cut out each circle, including the ones in the centers.

**12.** Attach the three circles to one another. Layer up in size order, applying a thin layer of glue to the back of each one and attaching it to the next, aligning the central holes. Once the three circles are glued to each other, glue them onto the house piece, aligning the central holes with the hole in the house.

**13.** Apply a thin layer of glue to the two roof faces of the house, then take the scalloped navy rectangle piece and press it onto the roof, aligning the long straight edge of the piece with the back edge of the house so that it overhangs only the front of the house.

**14.** Take the pale peach scalloped V-shaped piece. Apply a thin layer of glue to the back of the piece's two rectangular scalloped areas (not the triangular scalloped area in the center), and attach it to the top of the roof. Begin by pressing the tabbed face onto the side of the roof so that the tab folds over the top of the roof, then wrap the triangular face around the front of the roof before pressing down the final side, aligning the straight edges of the piece with the top and back of the roof.

**15.** Take the two creased gold shutter pieces. Apply a thin layer of glue to the back of the plain half of each piece, then tuck one around each side of the window and press them onto the back of the front face of the house. You will need to get your fingers through the window to press them in position while the glue begins to dry.

**16.** If your clock mechanism has specific instructions, follow them. If not, remove the hands from the clock mechanism. Attach double-sided self-adhesive foam pads to the front of the clock mechanism, avoiding the moving parts. Thread the center of the mechanism through the hole in the paper, from back to front, and press over the areas of the foam pads to secure into position. Reattach the clock hands.

**17.** Take the two hanging leaf pieces and fold over the top oval of each strip. Apply a small amount of glue to the folded section and press centrally onto the base of the house in the positions shown.

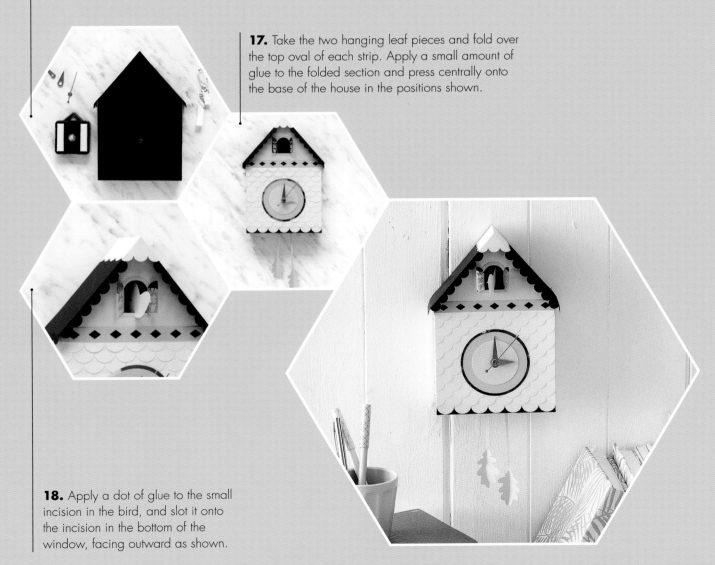

**18.** Apply a dot of glue to the small incision in the bird, and slot it onto the incision in the bottom of the window, facing outward as shown.

# 24

# PAPER PINEAPPLE

Inspired by their historical rarity, pineapples have long been a favored subject for designers and architects, symbolizing warmth, welcome, and luxury. As long as you take the time to get the combination of mountain and valley folds right, this exotic paper-engineered sculpture will add a tropical touch of art-deco glamour to your home.

## YOU WILL NEED

**1** 11¾ × 16½ in. (A3) sheet of light card in white
**2** 2 8¼ × 11¾ in. (A4) sheets of paper in pearlescent gold
**3** X-acto knife   **4** Cutting mat   **5** Metal ruler
**6** Scissors   **7** Embossing tool
**8** Bone folder   **9** Tacky glue

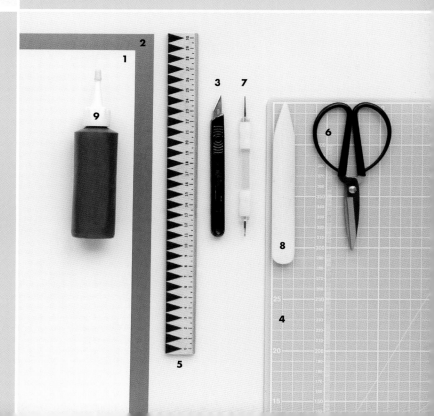

# TO MAKE

**2.** Use an embossing tool and ruler to score the fold lines. The fold lines are labeled on the template as being either valley or mountain folds. Use a bone folder to fold the mountain folds first, followed by the valley folds.

**1.** Using the corresponding templates (see page 134), cut out each piece as shown using an X-acto knife, cutting mat, and metal ruler where necessary, or use scissors if you prefer.

**3.** Place the creased piece in front of you, right-side up. Along the top is a row of trapezium shapes, each with a tab along its right edge. Work along the row, applying a thin layer of tacky glue to the front of each tab before attaching it to the back of the adjacent edge on the next trapezium. Repeat this along the bottom of the piece. You will now have a curved structure. One edge of the piece should be a zigzag, and the other straight. Position the zigzag edge on top of the straight edge, on the outside.

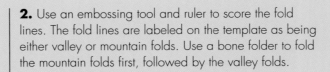

**4.** At the bottom of the piece is an octagon-shaped face. At this end, apply glue to the final trapezium tab and secure it to the back of the adjacent trapezium face, closing the shape. There will now be an octagon-shaped hole surrounded by seven tabs and an octagon-shaped face. Apply a thin layer of glue to each tab and press the octagon facedown onto the tabs, aligning the edges while the glue dries.

**5.** Apply glue to the back of the zigzag edge and press onto the paper beneath, aligning the creases. Glue the final trapezium tab to the back of the adjacent side to complete the shape.

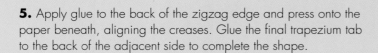

**6.** Use the blade of your scissors to gently curl each of the singular gold leaf-shaped pieces. Sort into groups of short leaves and longer leaves.

**7.** Stand the white piece up so that the open end is at the top, then take the short leaves. Apply a dot of glue to the rectangular end of the first leaf, then attach it to the inside of the white piece so that it curves outward, aligning the scored line on the leaf with the white top edge. Gently fold the leaf along the score line where it meets the white piece so that it stands upward. Repeat this with all remaining small leaves.

**8.** For this step you will need the longer single leaves. Take the first leaf and apply a thin layer of glue to the bottom ½ in. (1.5 cm) at the rectangular end. Place in the middle of the pineapple, fixing the leaf to the inside of one of the short leaves, curving outward and aligning the leaves at the base. Repeat this with all the remaining larger leaves.

### Color change
Try making your pineapple in gold paper for a brass pineapple look and all-out glamour, or in yellow with green leaves for a fun, tropical feel.

**9.** Take the strip of leaves and use the scissors to gently curl the tip of each leaf point upward. Apply a thin layer of glue to the back of the end leaf, then curve the piece around and attach the glued leaf to the front of the opposite end leaf, aligning the edges.

**10.** Apply a thin layer of glue to the bottom 1 in. (3 cm) of the leaf tube. Take the pineapple and spread the attached leaves slightly outward. Place the leaf cylinder in the center and push down to align the bases of the leaves. Push the single leaves back inward, then hold while the glue begins to dry, attaching the leaf cylinder in place.

## 25

# FESTIVAL CROWN

The perfect accessory for a celebration—
whether a wedding, party, or festival—
this crepe-paper crown will stay
beautiful for as long as you need it to,
unlike real flowers, and is easier to
make than its detail might suggest.

## YOU WILL NEED

Roll of heavyweight crepe paper in:
**1** navy  **2** white
**3** pale blue green  **4** green
**5** Metal ruler  **6** Scissors
**7** White acrylic paint  **8** Paintbrush
**9** 8 polystyrene balls, ²/₅ in. (1 cm) diameter
**10** Tacky glue  **11** Pliers with wire cutters
**12** 12 light-gauge green floral wires,
12 in. (30 cm)  **13** Hot glue gun
**14** Green floral tape  **15** 16 polystyrene
balls, ³/₅ in. (1.5 cm) diameter
**16** 2 heavy-gauge green floral
wires, 12 in. (30 cm)

# TO MAKE

**1.** Measuring with a ruler, cut eight 3 × ¾ in. (8 × 2 cm) strips of navy crepe paper across the grain. Paint the front of each strip of crepe with white acrylic paint, leaving a visible navy edge, then leave to dry. Use scissors to fringe along the navy edge, making cuts close together as shown, cutting down to around ¼ in. (7 mm) from the end.

**2.** Cut eight pieces of navy crepe paper large enough to wrap around a ⅖ in. (1 cm) polystyrene ball. Apply dots of tacky glue to the first piece of crepe paper and stretch it around the first ball, twisting the excess crepe paper into a stalk. Once the glue is dry, trim off the stalk with scissors. Repeat with the remaining balls.

**3.** Use pliers with wire cutters to cut four light-gauge floral wires in half. Use a glue gun to apply a tiny amount of glue to one end of the first half wire, then immediately push a crepe-covered ball onto the end, inserting the wire into the side where the excess crepe was trimmed and pushing to around halfway through the ball. Repeat with each ball.

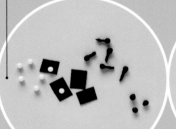

### Variation
Try altering the flower styles—the construction method used for this floral crown could be adapted for any paper-flower crown or even a wreath.

**4.** Use the glue gun to apply a line of hot glue along the base of the first fringed strip, then immediately wrap it around the base of the first ball. Repeat with each fringed strip.

**5.** Take the white and pale blue crepe papers and use the corresponding template (see page 135) to cut out 24 petal pieces in each color. The petals need to be cut along the grain of the crepe, meaning that the small folds of the crepe run from the top of each petal to the bottom. It can help speed up the cutting to cut out a strip of paper 2 in. (5 cm) high across the grain of the crepe first, then accordian-fold the strip a couple of times, and cut a few petals at once.

**6.** Stretch the crepe petals slightly by holding the petal with your thumb in the center and gently pulling the paper out to the sides to slightly cup the petal.

**7.** Separate the petals by color. Take the first three petals in one color and one of the fringed wires. Use the glue gun to apply glue to the base of the first petal and attach it to the base of the fringe. Continue with the remaining two petals, evenly spacing the petals around the stamen. Repeat with the remaining fringed wires, making four white and four blue flowers.

**8.** Repeat Step 7 with the remaining petals, attaching three more petals in the same color to each flower and positioning each petal in between the previously glued petals.

**9.** Take the green crepe paper. Cut out 24 freehand pointed ellipse shapes measuring approximately ⅓ × 1½ in. (0.75 × 4 cm), along the grain of the crepe. Glue three of these pieces around the base of each flower, positioning each ellipse down the center of a petal, half over the petal and half over the wire. Repeat with each flower.

**10.** Wrap the wire in floral tape, stretching the tape as you wrap. Begin by wrapping around the green crepe and continue all the way to the end of the wire; then repeat with each flower.

**11.** Cut eight pieces of light blue crepe paper large enough to wrap around a ⅗ in. (1.5 cm) polystyrene ball. Do the same with white crepe paper. Apply a dot of tacky glue to a piece of paper and stretch it around a ball, twisting the excess crepe paper into a stalk. Repeat with the remaining balls.

**12.** Use the template to cut out 16 leaf shapes from green crepe paper, along the grain of the crepe. Stretch the crepe slightly in the center of each leaf: hold the leaf with your thumbs in the center and gently pull the paper out to the sides to cup the leaf.

### Hone your skills
When working with floral tape, stretch the tape as you wrap to release the glue in the tape and allow it to stick to itself.

**13.** Use the wire cutters to cut the remaining eight light-gauge wires in half. Use the glue gun to apply hot glue to one end of the first half wire, then immediately push against the stalk of a crepe-covered ball. Apply hot glue to the bottom tip of a leaf and immediately push against the previously glued wire so that the wire is sandwiched between the ball stalk and the leaf, and the leaf cups around the ball.

**14.** Take two of the wires glued in Step 13. Wrap the top half of the first wire with floral tape, stretching as you wrap, then cut the tape. Take your second wire and again begin wrapping with floral tape from the top. Once you get a third of the way down, add in the first half-wrapped stem and continue to wrap, binding the wires together.

**15.** Take the two heavy-gauge floral wires and twist them together at the ends to make a ring that fits around your head.

**16.** Arrange the flowers and buds·around your wire ring to roughly plan the placement. Bind each wire to the ring with a small amount of floral tape. At this stage, just attach a tiny section of each piece to the ring so that you can tweak the positions if required.

**Customize it**
The petal, leaf, and ellipse shapes in this project do not need to be totally accurate—small inconsistencies could even add to the overall aesthetic, making it look more natural.

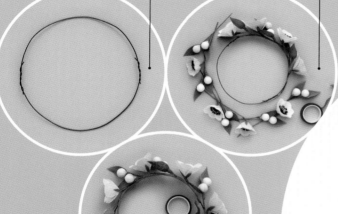

**17.** Once all of the stems are roughly attached to the ring, even out the placement of the stems, then wrap all the way around the ring, binding the stems to the ring using floral tape. Separate the flowers and buds.

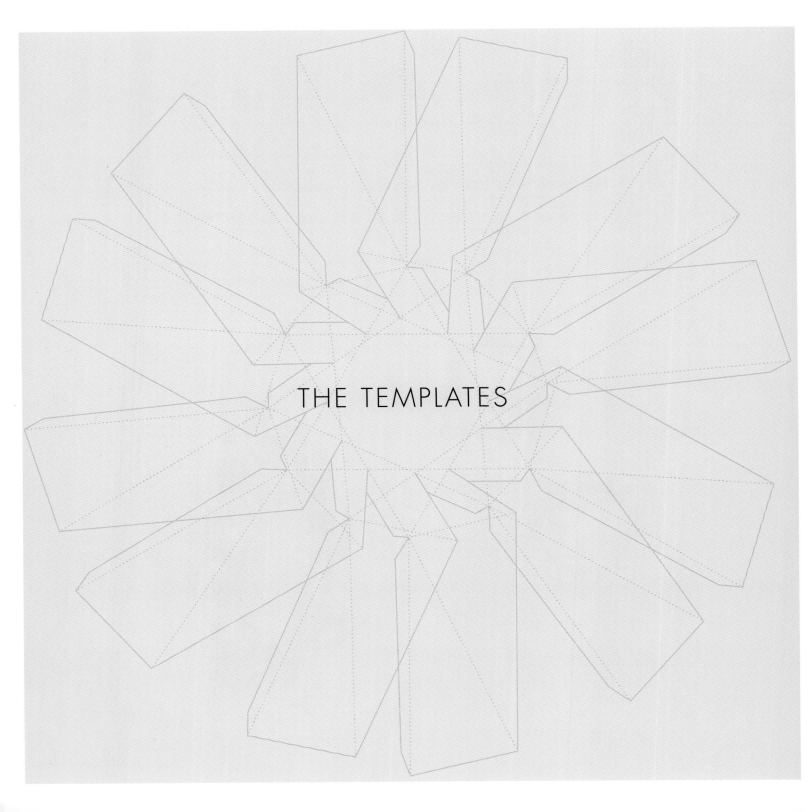

THE TEMPLATES

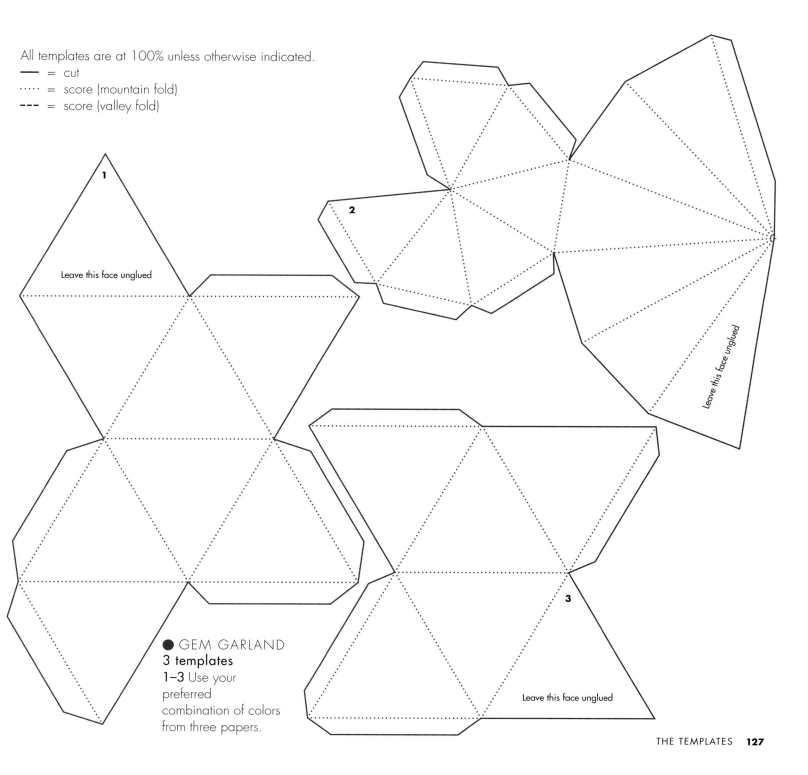

All templates are at 100% unless otherwise indicated.

—— = cut

········ = score (mountain fold)

--- = score (valley fold)

1

Leave this face unglued

2

Leave this face unglued

3

Leave this face unglued

● GEM GARLAND
3 templates
1–3 Use your preferred combination of colors from three papers.

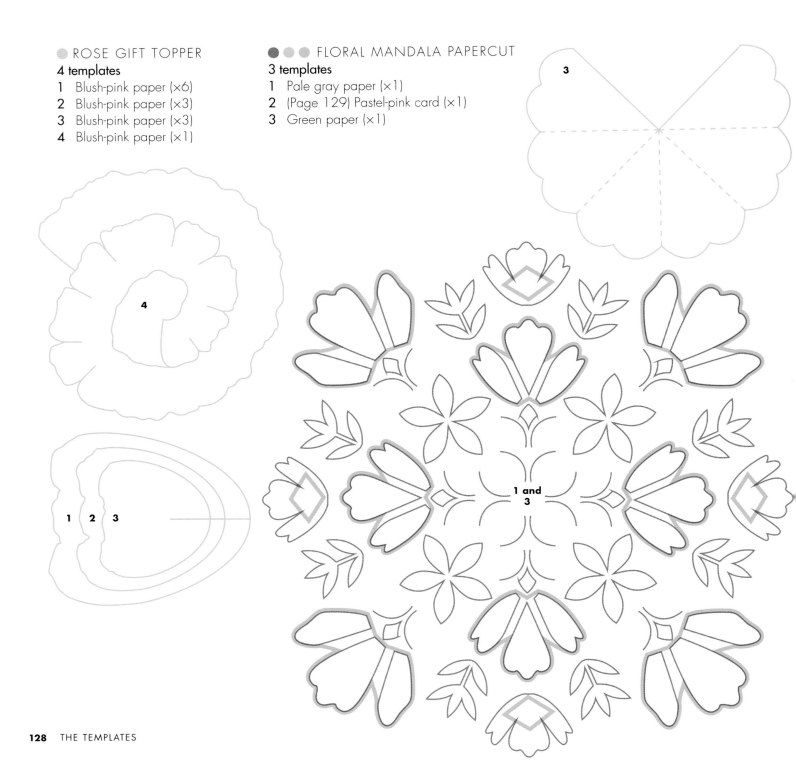

## ● ROSE GIFT TOPPER

**4 templates**

1  Blush-pink paper (×6)
2  Blush-pink paper (×3)
3  Blush-pink paper (×3)
4  Blush-pink paper (×1)

## ● ●● ● FLORAL MANDALA PAPERCUT

**3 templates**

1  Pale gray paper (×1)
2  (Page 129) Pastel-pink card (×1)
3  Green paper (×1)

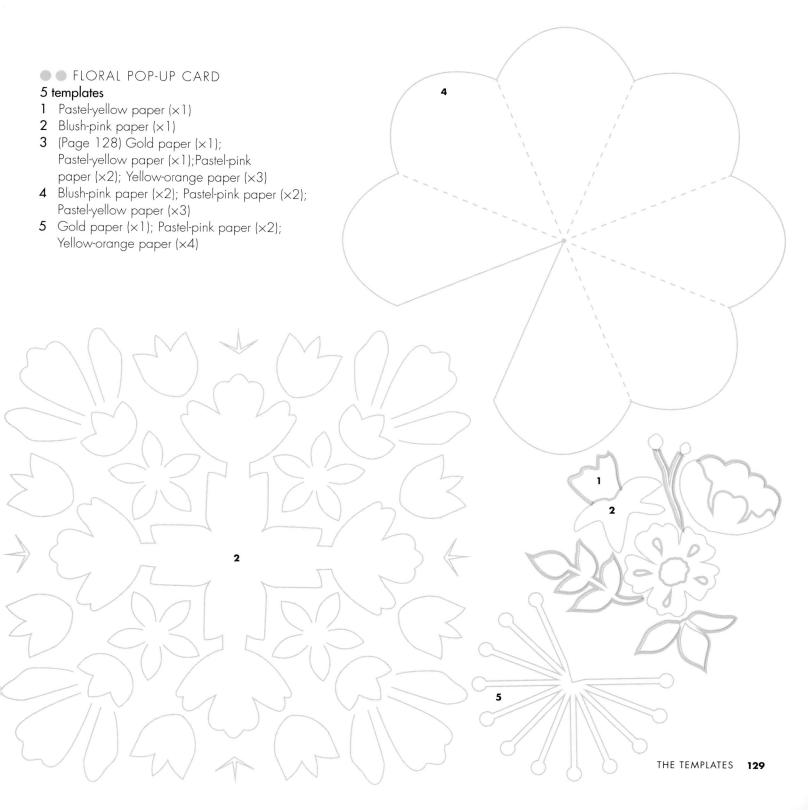

## FLORAL POP-UP CARD

### 5 templates

1. Pastel-yellow paper (×1)
2. Blush-pink paper (×1)
3. (Page 128) Gold paper (×1);
   Pastel-yellow paper (×1); Pastel-pink
   paper (×2); Yellow-orange paper (×3)
4. Blush-pink paper (×2); Pastel-pink paper (×2);
   Pastel-yellow paper (×3)
5. Gold paper (×1); Pastel-pink paper (×2);
   Yellow-orange paper (×4)

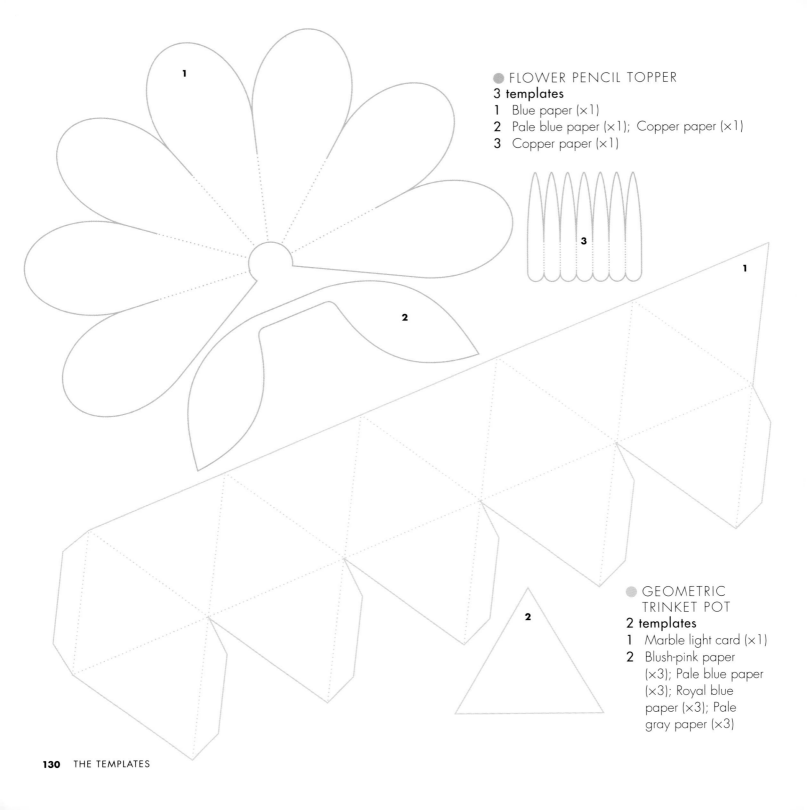

● FLOWER PENCIL TOPPER
**3 templates**
1   Blue paper (×1)
2   Pale blue paper (×1); Copper paper (×1)
3   Copper paper (×1)

● GEOMETRIC
TRINKET POT
**2 templates**
1   Marble light card (×1)
2   Blush-pink paper
    (×3); Pale blue paper
    (×3); Royal blue
    paper (×3); Pale
    gray paper (×3)

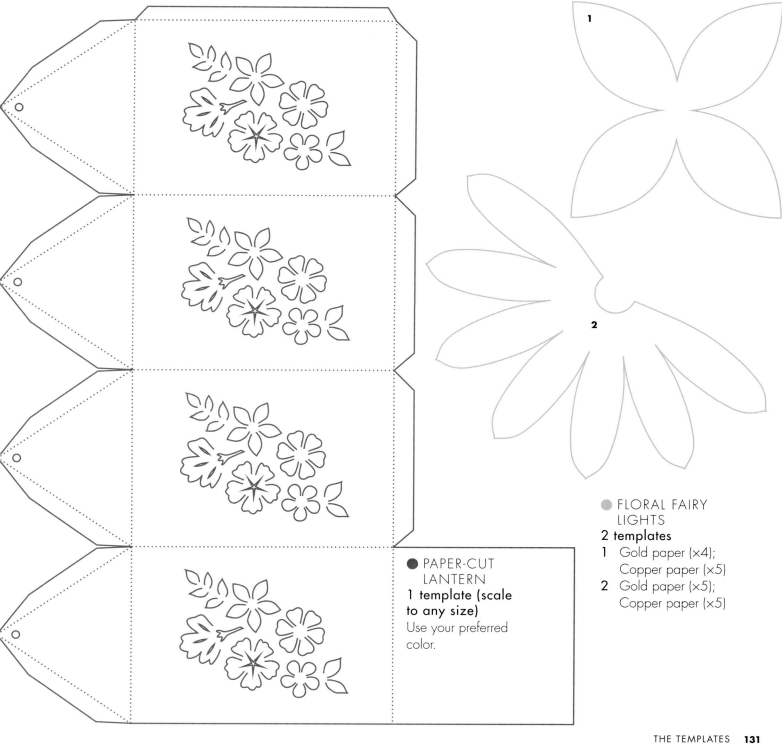

● PAPER-CUT
LANTERN
**1 template (scale to any size)**
Use your preferred color.

● FLORAL FAIRY
LIGHTS
**2 templates**
1  Gold paper (×4);
   Copper paper (×5)
2  Gold paper (×5);
   Copper paper (×5)

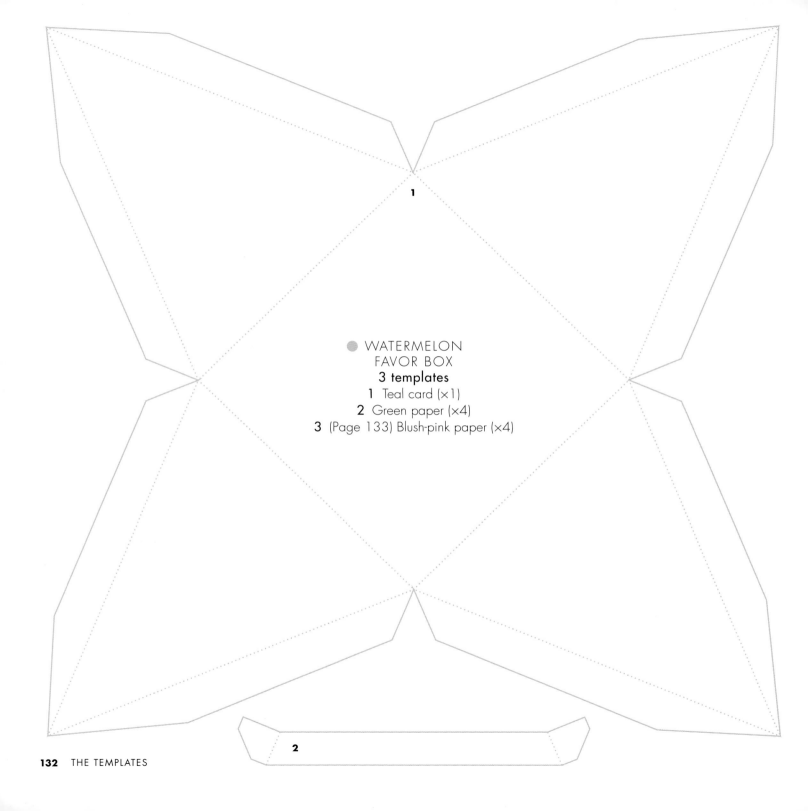

**1**

● WATERMELON
FAVOR BOX
**3 templates**
**1** Teal card (×1)
**2** Green paper (×4)
**3** (Page 133) Blush-pink paper (×4)

**2**

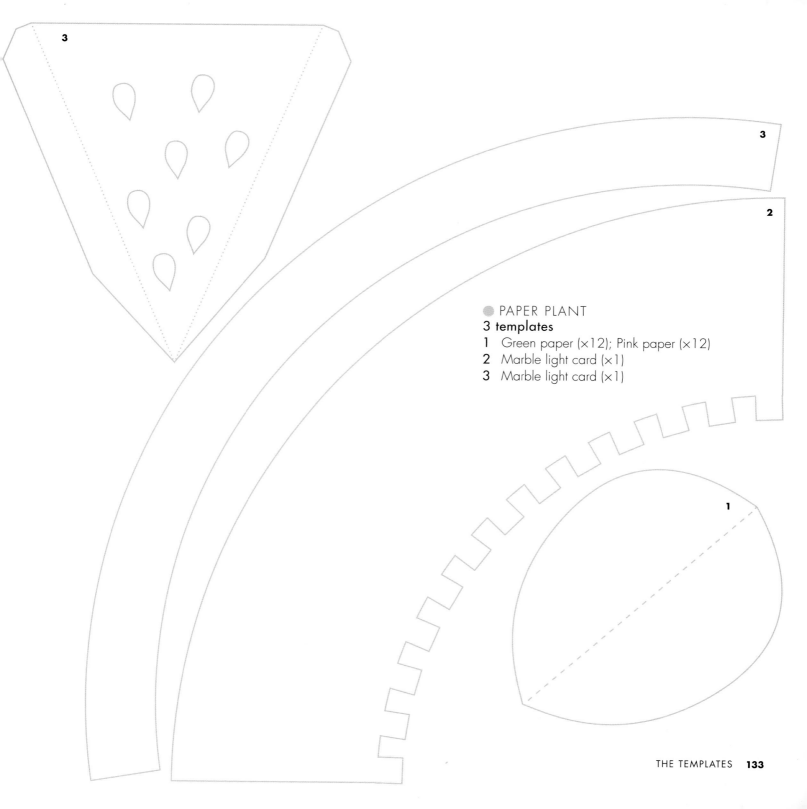

**3**

**3**

**2**

● PAPER PLANT
**3 templates**
1   Green paper (×12); Pink paper (×12)
2   Marble light card (×1)
3   Marble light card (×1)

**1**

## PAPER PINEAPPLE

**4 templates**
**(scale all templates by 200%)**

1 White light card (×1)
2 Gold paper (×1)
3 Gold paper (×8)
4 Gold paper (×8)

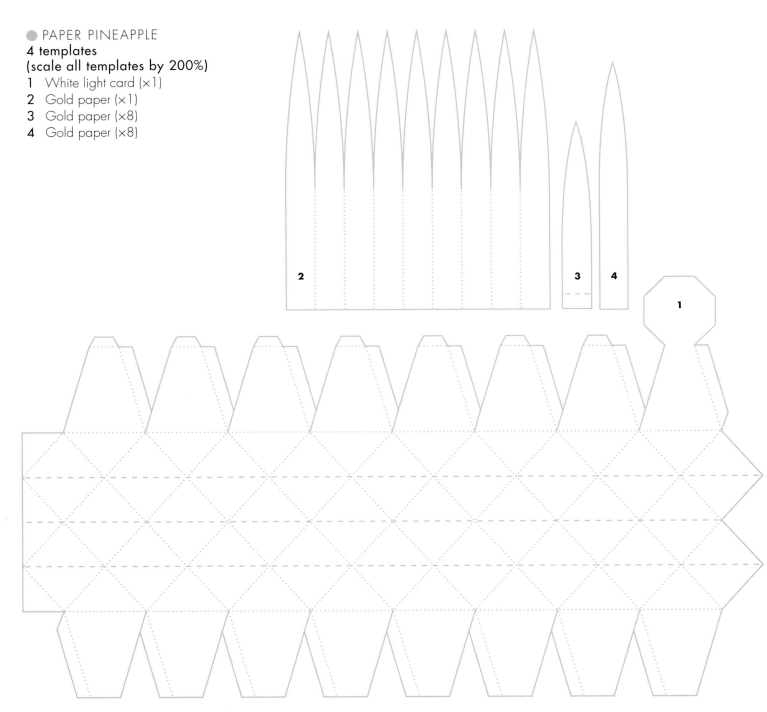

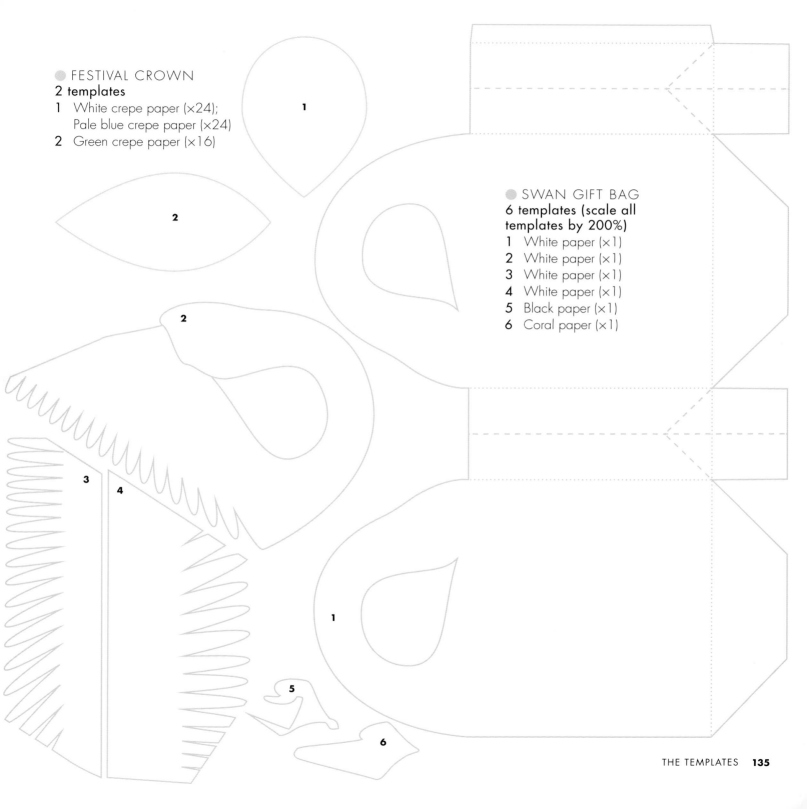

## FESTIVAL CROWN
**2 templates**
1 White crepe paper (×24);
  Pale blue crepe paper (×24)
2 Green crepe paper (×16)

## SWAN GIFT BAG
**6 templates (scale all templates by 200%)**
1 White paper (×1)
2 White paper (×1)
3 White paper (×1)
4 White paper (×1)
5 Black paper (×1)
6 Coral paper (×1)

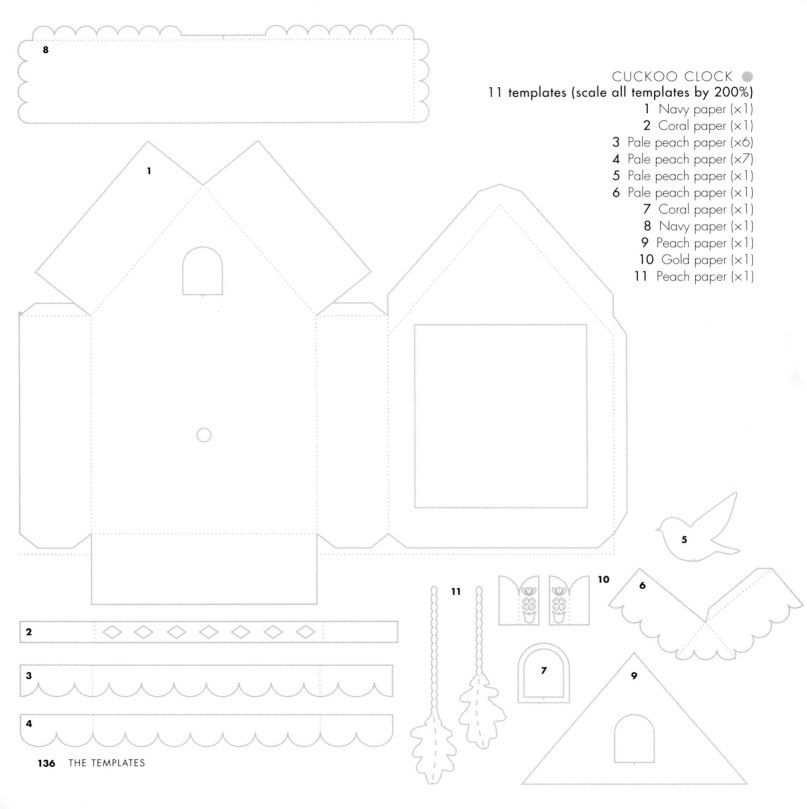

CUCKOO CLOCK ●

11 templates (scale all templates by 200%)

1 Navy paper (×1)
2 Coral paper (×1)
3 Pale peach paper (×6)
4 Pale peach paper (×7)
5 Pale peach paper (×1)
6 Pale peach paper (×1)
7 Coral paper (×1)
8 Navy paper (×1)
9 Peach paper (×1)
10 Gold paper (×1)
11 Peach paper (×1)

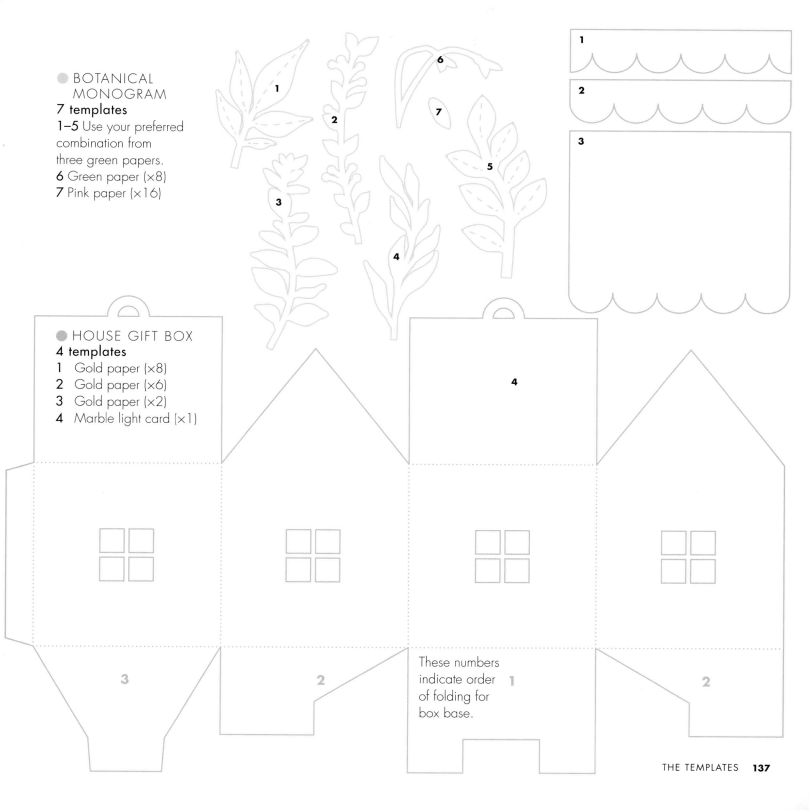

● BOTANICAL
  MONOGRAM
**7 templates**
**1–5** Use your preferred
combination from
three green papers.
**6** Green paper (×8)
**7** Pink paper (×16)

● HOUSE GIFT BOX
**4 templates**
**1** Gold paper (×8)
**2** Gold paper (×6)
**3** Gold paper (×2)
**4** Marble light card (×1)

These numbers
indicate order
of folding for
box base.

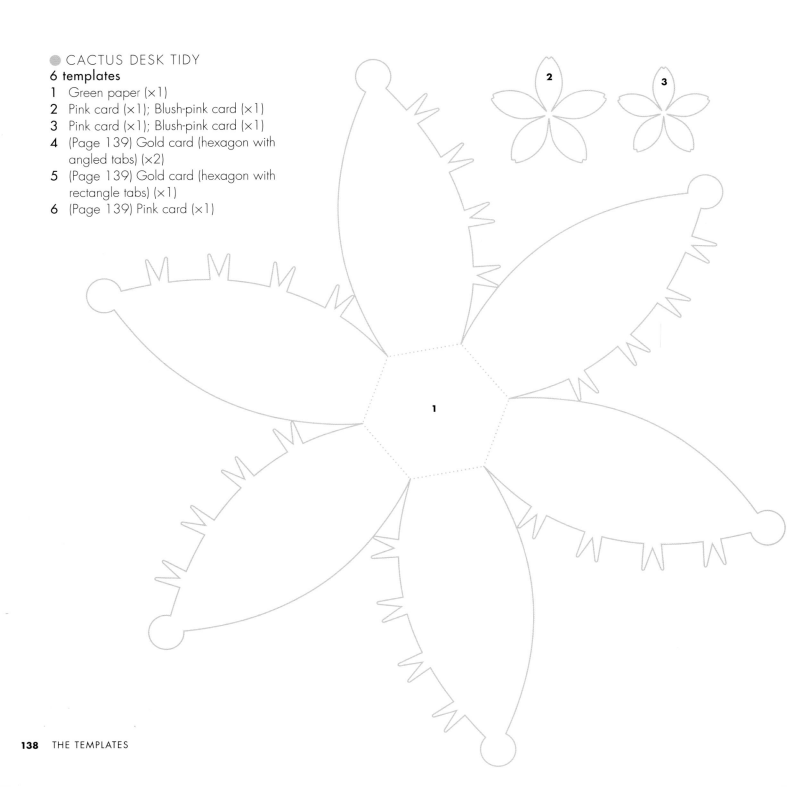

● CACTUS DESK TIDY
### 6 templates
1  Green paper (×1)
2  Pink card (×1); Blush-pink card (×1)
3  Pink card (×1); Blush-pink card (×1)
4  (Page 139) Gold card (hexagon with angled tabs) (×2)
5  (Page 139) Gold card (hexagon with rectangle tabs) (×1)
6  (Page 139) Pink card (×1)

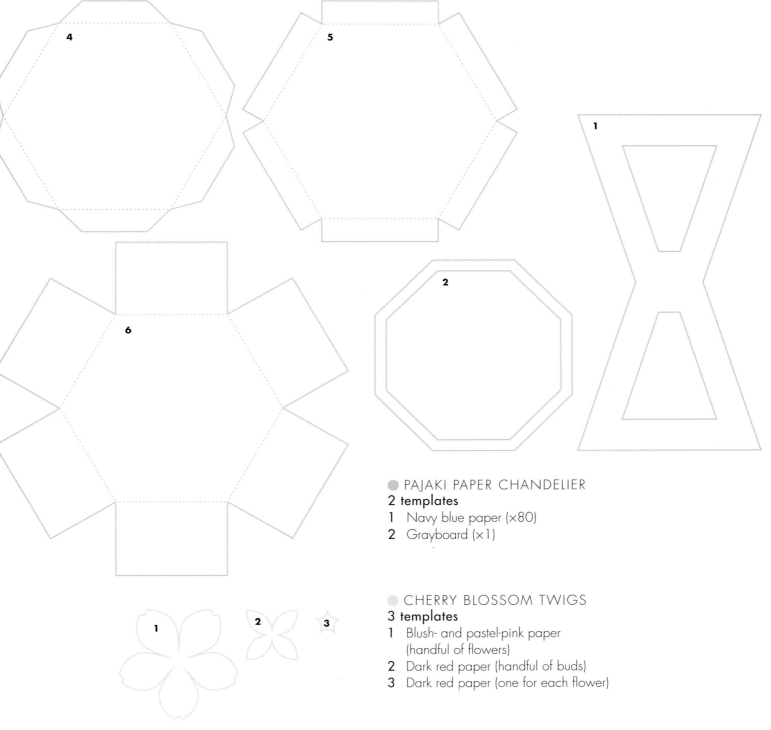

● PAJAKI PAPER CHANDELIER

**2 templates**
1 Navy blue paper (×80)
2 Grayboard (×1)

● CHERRY BLOSSOM TWIGS

**3 templates**
1 Blush- and pastel-pink paper
  (handful of flowers)
2 Dark red paper (handful of buds)
3 Dark red paper (one for each flower)

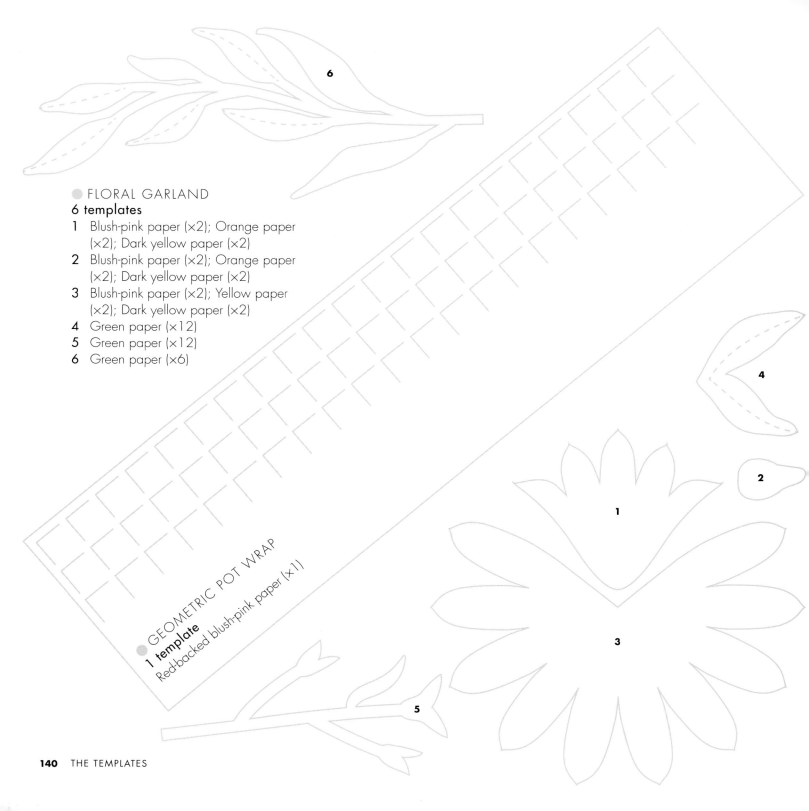

## FLORAL GARLAND

### 6 templates

1   Blush-pink paper (×2); Orange paper
    (×2); Dark yellow paper (×2)
2   Blush-pink paper (×2); Orange paper
    (×2); Dark yellow paper (×2)
3   Blush-pink paper (×2); Yellow paper
    (×2); Dark yellow paper (×2)
4   Green paper (×12)
5   Green paper (×12)
6   Green paper (×6)

## GEOMETRIC POT WRAP
### 1 template
Red-backed blush-pink paper (×1)

## MINIMAL VASE
**1 template (scale by 128%)**
Light card (×1)
Use your preferred color.

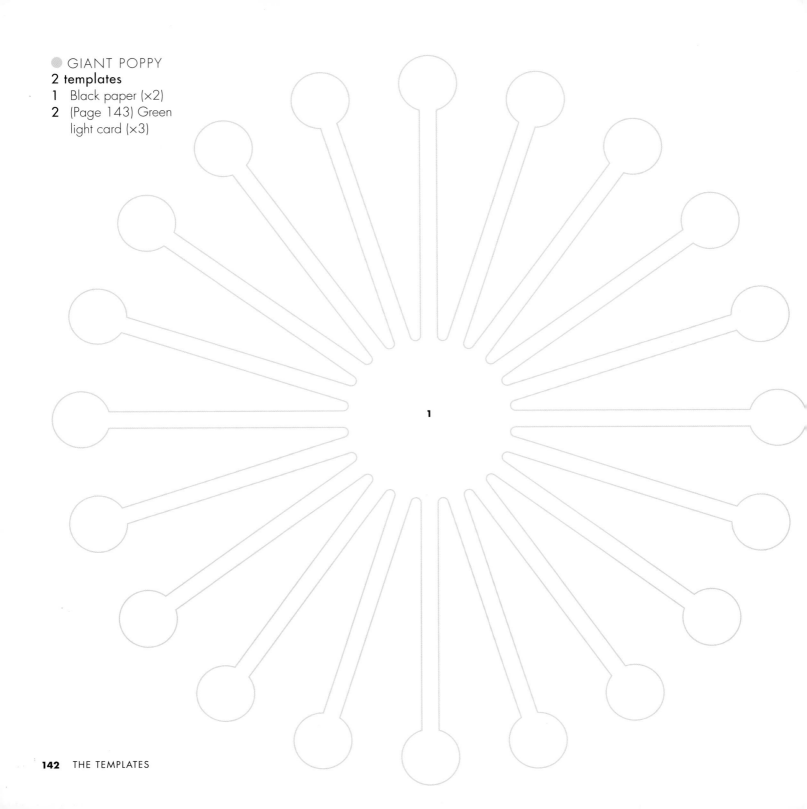

● GIANT POPPY
**2 templates**
1   Black paper (×2)
2   (Page 143) Green
     light card (×3)

1

FLORAL CAKE
TOPPERS
3 templates
1  Green vellum (×1)
2  Colored vellum (×1)
3  Colored vellum (×1)

# INDEX

Illustrations are in *italics*. Projects are in **bold**. Templates are indicated by the use of "t."

**A**

adhesive, all-purpose *12, 13*

**B**

bone folder *12, 13*
**Botanical Monogram** *24–27, 25–26, 137t*
bow tying *17, 17*

**C**

**Cactus Desk Tidy** 90, *90–95, 92–95, 138–39t*
card, types of *10, 11*
**Cherry Blossom Twigs** *46–49, 47–49, 139t*
colored card *10, 11*
colored paper *10, 11*
crepe paper *10, 11*
**Cuckoo Clock** *110–15, 111–15, 136t*
curling *16, 16*
cutting *14, 14*
cutting mat *12, 13*
cylinder *16, 16*

**E**

embossing tool *12, 13*
erasers *12, 13*

**F**

**Festival Crown** *120–25, 121–25, 135t*
**Floral Cake Toppers** *54–57, 55–57, 143t*
**Floral Fairy Lights** 38, *38–41, 40–41, 131t*
**Floral Garland** 101, *101–4, 103–4, 140t*
**Floral Mandala Papercut** *20–23, 20–23, 128–29t*
**Floral Pop-Up Card** 68, *68–72, 70–72, 129t, 128t*
floral tape *12, 13*
floral wire *10, 11*

**Flower Pencil Topper** 50, *50–53, 52–53, 130t*
foam board *10, 11*
folder, bone *12, 13*
folding *15, 15*

**G**

**Gem Garland** *80–82, 80–83, 127t*
**Geometric Pot Wrap** *73–74, 73–75*
**Geometric Trinket Pot** *66–67, 66–67, 130t*
**Giant Poppy** 96, *96–100, 98–100, 142–43t*
glue, tacky *12, 13*

**H**

hole punch *12, 13*
hot glue gun *12, 13*
**House Gift Box** *32–35, 33–35, 137t*

**K**

knife, X-acto *12, 13*

**M**

materials *10, 11*
metallic card *10, 11*
metallic paper *10, 11*
**Minimal Vase** *36–37, 36–37, 141t*

**N**

needles, tapestry *12, 13*

**O**

**Origami Lampshade** 76, *78–79, 76–79*

**P**

paint *10, 11*
paintbrushes *12, 13*
**Pajaki Paper Chandelier** *105–8, 105–9, 139t*
**Paper-Cut Lantern** *28–31, 29–31, 131t*
**Paper Pineapple** *116–19,*

*117–19, 134t*
**Paper Plant** *84–89, 85–89, 133t*
paper, types of *10, 11*
pencil *12, 13*
pliers *12, 13*

**R**

ribbon *10, 11, 17, 17*
**Rose Gift Topper** *58–61, 59–61, 128t*
ruler, metal *12, 13*

**S**

scissors *12, 13, 16, 16*
scoring *15, 15*
skewers, wooden *16, 16*
staplers *12, 13*
**Swan Gift Bag** *42–45, 43–45, 135t*

**T**

tape *10, 11, 12, 13*
tape, double-sided *12, 13*
tapestry needles *12, 13*
techniques, basic *14–17*
tissue paper, colored *10, 11*
tools *12, 13*
tracing paper *10, 11*

**V**

vellum *10, 11*

**W**

washi tape *10, 11*
**Watermelon Favor Box** *62–65, 63–65, 132–33t*
wire cutters *12, 13*

**X**

X-acto knife *12, 13*

## AUTHOR'S ACKNOWLEDGMENTS

I have such a huge amount of gratitude for the support and love I have been given throughout this process.

Thank you so much to Julia, Philippa, Kate, Claire, Sam, and the whole wonderful team at Quarto for taking a chance on me, guiding me through this process, and giving me the opportunity to make a big tick on my bucket list.

My heartfelt thanks to my parents for your endless love, pride, belief, and encouragement, for helping me keep every other aspect of my life in line during this adventure, and for putting up with the mess that came with it! Mum, you encouraged all things creative from when I was old enough to hold a crayon, and without you I may not be on this path. Dad and Denise, without your immense support with my house I wouldn't have been able to keep my head above water during the creation of this book. I love you all.

My love and thanks to Preston, for your ongoing belief in me and for encouraging me to pursue my dreams. You knew I could make this work. Thank you for allowing me to have the biggest spare room to make a papery mess in and for reminding me to look after myself amidst the madness.

Thank you to Victoria, Rosie, Becki, Annick, Hanni, Fran, and all my incredible friends who uplift me when I need it most and have been so kind about the book. Your support has kept me going! Thank you to Lusea for sharing my brain and always bringing a smile to my face, to Georgie and Amy D. for believing in me a lot more than I believe in myself, and to Dana for your infectious positivity, excitement, and kind words from the other side of the world. I'm so happy that I crossed paths with all of you.

Finally, thank you from the bottom of my heart to everyone I have worked with and to all who have followed my journey, cheering me on from the sidelines. You have allowed me to do what I love.